Anxiety

How to Retrain Your Brain to Eliminate Anxiety, Depression and Phobias Using Cognitive Behavioral Therapy, and Develop Better Self-Awareness and Relationships with Emotional Intelligence

By

Ryan James

Table of Contents

Book – I: Emotional Intelligence: The Complete Step by Step Guide on Self Awareness, Controlling Your Emotions and Improving Your EQ

Book - II: Emotional Intelligence: 21 Most Effective Tips and Tricks on Self Awareness, Controlling Your Emotions, and Improving Your EQ

Book - III: Cognitive Behavioral Therapy: The Definitive Guide to Understanding Your Brain, Depression, Anxiety and How to Over Come It

Book - IV: Cognitive Behavioral Therapy: Mastery- How to Master Your Brain & Your Emotions to Overcome Depression, Anxiety and Phobias

Book – I

Emotional Intelligence

The Complete Step-by-Step Guide on Self-Awareness, Controlling Your Emotions and Improving Your EQ

Introduction: A Step-by-Step Guide to Developing Emotional Intelligence

To define emotional intelligence (EI) as being aware of one's emotions and knowing how to control those emotions to build fruitful and empathetic relationships doesn't give you the full picture. The beauty in studying EI is to understand how to develop and use that emotional intelligence to improve your life. My goal in this book is to take you through the steps of how to do just that—to identify, develop and heighten your emotional intelligence to create stronger personal and professional relationships.

For clarity, let's take emotional intelligence beyond its definition and step into a greater understanding of what EI can do for you. Perhaps the best way to bring clarity to the term "emotional intelligence" is first to dispel some of its mysteries and myths. Emotional intelligence is NOT a personality trait. People who have high EI aren't necessarily optimistic, agreeable, or always happy. EI goes deeper than your outward personality; it's almost like having an inherent ability to perceive emotions and respond in a way that benefits all parties. It's learning how to feel emotions, not just be able to identify or recognize them. Having high emotional intelligence is knowing how to harness emotional energy and turn it into predictable and positive outcomes.

In my book, *Emotional Intelligence: The Definitive Guide to Understanding Your Emotions, How to Improve Your EQ and Your Relationships,* I spent lots of time describing the term and the importance it played in your personal and professional relationships. So, for some of you, it might be a good idea to first read that book and my second book *Emotional Intelligence Mastery: How to Master Your Emotions, Improve Your EQ, and Massively Improve Your Relationships*. They both offer a firm foundation on what is introduced in this book. Now that you've learned what Emotional Intelligence is and how it can influence your life, we're going to take you through a step-by-step guided tour of how to improve your emotional intelligence through a robust analysis of your emotions and that of those with whom you surround yourself.

In this step-by-step guide to emotional intelligence, you'll learn how to assess your EI, observe others emotions with a heightened awareness, practice control and focus on improving your EI, and create predictable outcomes that bring you greater success in life. Instead of ignoring or scoffing at the evidence of emotions, you'll learn how to follow the steps to change the course of your life and others by using those same emotions to make you more decisive and attractive.

Often, the best way to better understand a topic is to begin questioning your feelings on the matter. So, let's get personal, shall we? Let's make it all about you. Ask yourself the following:

1. What will develop a high emotional intelligence in you?

2. How will you know if you have a high emotional intelligence?

3. Why is it important to know what your emotional intelligence is, anyway?

4. When will you notice a difference in your life?

5. Where can you expect this greater emotional awareness to take you?

To know what developing a high emotional intelligence can do for you, it's helpful to know what it has done for others. Developing a high emotional intelligence has helped CEOs run huge corporations, national leaders gain public support, and creative artists reflect the values and truths of their times. As you work through the steps of this book, you'll begin to examine your personal EI and determine the things you'll need to do to climb to a higher standard of emotional communications. Some of you who already have high EI may not notice a significant difference, merely a little improvement here and there to lighten the load. However, those of you who have been ruled for decades by emotional outbursts or suffered social isolation because of poor EI, the changes you'll experience will be immediate.

As to where you can expect this greater emotional awareness to take you? Well, the possibilities are limited only by your ability to practice these steps daily to become an emotional intelligence mensa. Improving your EI can lead you to more stable relationships, greater professional achievements and a more intuitive understanding of how to respond to others and predict how they will react to you. In short, increasing your emotional intelligence can be life altering.

You don't have to be a road scholar to have high emotional intelligence. In fact, there is no correlation between having a high IQ and a high EI. The size of your brain has little to do with your ability to recognize and build your emotional intelligence. It's more about the size of your heart than the size of your brain. When you approach others, how do you perceive them? What feelings do you leave them with when they leave your presence? It's more about feeling with your heart than knowing with your mind. That's what the following steps will show you—how to control and apply your feelings and emotions so that you will be perceived and will see others in their absolute best light.

As you learn and follow the steps presented in this book, you'll begin to see yourself and others differently. Instead of jumping to conclusions before knowing all the facts of the situation, you'll find yourself stepping back and observing the other person's emotions. When, before, you would have made a rash decision based on irrational feelings, now you'll start to mull things over a bit more and imagine how your behavior might negatively impact others. That's called having emotional intelligence. So, join me on this tour, this step-by-step guide to helping you discover and develop your emotional intelligence.

Chapter 1: Step #1—Assessing Your Emotional Intelligence

If we can agree that Emotional Intelligence is important, how can you assess your EI? We have designed a little test for you that will give you an accurate idea of your Emotional Intelligence. Take a few moments to answer the follow questions, and then let's talk about your scores.

Emotional Intelligence Assessment

Answer the following questions and then tally up your score. At the end of the test, you'll know your Emotional Intelligence level.

1.   You're riding in a taxi. You notice that the driver is taking many side streets, and you fear your charge will reflect his poor sense of direction. What do you do?

   a.   Tap him on the shoulder and tell him you don't appreciate his attempt to rack up a higher tab.

   b.   Let him know you are familiar with the area and ask him what he believes is the quickest route to take to get to your destination.

   c.   Ignore him and decide never to use this company again.

   d.   Refuse to pay the bill.

2.   Your daughter has a friend in the neighborhood come over to play. When the friend leaves, your little girl begins to cry because she has no more money in her piggy bank. It appears the older child next door took advantage of your daughter and stole the money from her piggy bank. What would you do?

   a.   Listen to your daughter's story, and then share with her how something similar happened to you when you were little so she wouldn't feel so bad.

   b.   March right over to the neighbor's house with your daughter to tell the girl's mother and demand she gives back the money.

     c.   Let your little girl express her anger over her loss, and then together discover a way to prevent this from ever happening again.

     d.   Reprimand your daughter and refuse to give her any more allowance until she learns to take better care of her money.

3.   You are trying to impress your boss and win the "salesperson of the year" award, but you're getting discouraged because the last 20 calls you've made have been hang-ups. What do you do?

     a.   Try a different call tactic.

     b.   Quit

     c.   Stop trying to get so much attention for your performance.

     d.   Stop and consider what you are doing that could be hindering your opportunity to make the sale, and then try something you've learned that might be more efficient.

4.   You're on your way to the movies with your significant other, and the driver in the car next to you cuts you off. Your significant other starts to fume—what do you do?

     a.   Encourage him to pull beside the other drive so you can yell obscenities.

     b.   Turn the radio up and sing to drown out your partner's swearing.

     c.   Tell him he gets way too mad when drivers cut him off, and then share with him how it happens to you all the time and you don't lose it.

     d.   Let him express himself, and then point out that the other driver could have been an out-of-towner or someone headed for the hospital.

5.   You are trying to learn some new software on your computer, but the tutorial is not helping, and you're getting quite frustrated. What do you do?

     a.   You give it a rest for a while, and then ask a friend who is good with computers for help.

b.   You vow never to use the computer again and shut it down.

c.   You decide to wait until you're in a better mood to try learning the new program.

d.   You choose to take a class on the software and be patient with yourself during the learning curve.

Scoring: Give yourself five points for every correct answer.

1.   Correct answer is b = 5 Points

2.   Correct answer is c = 5 Points

3.   Correct answer is d = 5 Points

4.   Correct answer is d = 5 Points

5.   Correct answer is d = 5 Points

If you scored 25 points, you have the highest Emotional Intelligence.

If you scored 20 points, you have more Emotional Intelligence than many.

If you scored 15 points, you need to work on your Emotional Intelligence.

If you scored 10 points or below, you have little awareness of your or others' emotions.

So, let's think about this brief assessment for a moment. How do you "feel" about the emotions this test stirred in you? What if I told you, no exact five-question test could demonstrate the level of your emotional intelligence? The five-question assessment has no validity, but now you're probably feeling a whole other set of emotions. You could be feeling frustration, confusion, tricked even. Any way you look at it, there are some emotions you have to deal with right now. So, now we can truly assess how you're thinking about these emotions.

Most people tend to over-rate their Emotional Intelligence level. Have you ever had bosses who considered themselves to be very tuned into their emotions and those of their employees, but who were actually living in an emotional wasteland? All this thinking about emotions leads us to a different definition of Emotional Intelligence. Emotional Intelligence is how you think about and express your feelings. Taking it one step further, how do you use that information about your feelings to change your behavior and the behavior of others?

Taking a test isn't going to provide answers about feelings and emotions. Contemplating your feelings and how to control your emotions is what will give you an accurate gauge on your Emotional Intelligence. Not all emotions are black or white—many fill up that gray area of complex feelings that need more than a label to define them. For example, it's easy to identify a feeling of sorrow when your pet dies. However, can you distinguish the difference between frustration and anger? Do you know when you're feeling shame or is it embarrassment you're experiencing?

Complex emotions need reflection and thought to sort through and assess. That reflection is what eventually improves and strengthens your Emotional Intelligence. Learning to deal productively with your emotions helps you to identify and assess others emotions. Emotions are not to be confused with moods. Moods are, by nature, flighty and erratic. Emotions are truer, easier to think through and assess. Have you ever awakened in a bad mood, as if for no reason? You've had no conversation, no event yet in your day that could cause you emotional turmoil—you're just in a mood, right? It's helpful to understand as we go through these steps that we're not speaking of mood swings here, but rather discussing one's inner emotions.

Since Emotional Intelligence requires thought about your feelings, let's do that to develop a more accurate measurement of your EI. I'm going to give you some situations, and I want you to think about how you typically feel when you find yourself enmeshed in them. The first step in assessing your feelings is simply recognizing or identifying them.

What did you feel when...

- Your best friend, once again, stood you up for a get-together?
- Your employer broke his/her promise to give you a pay increase?
- Your family member was very ill and in the hospital?

- You heard someone at your door at midnight, and you were all by yourself?
- Your significant other said they had a confession to make?
- Your mother or father expressed pride in your achievement?
- You wanted something so desperately but knew you could never have it?
- You lost your job or failed to get that promotion?
- Your sister or brother received rewards for something you knew you could do better?
- Your husband or wife forgot your birthday?

As you go through these issues, you will notice that some emotions are clearly defined, and others fall in that gray area. Emotions that you must think about are usually ones with layers of unresolved issues, ones that you have repeatedly stuffed down or ignored so as not to have to deal with them. By not pausing at the time to think through your emotions, you have stunted the forward progress of your Emotional Intelligence.

Assessing your Emotional Intelligence means asking yourself if you truly have a handle on your feelings. When you are emotional, do you react or stop to think things through? If your friend is hurting, do you avoid her company until she has worked through her problem, or do you stand by her and help her to resolve the emotional issue? All this is a part of your Emotional Intelligence. Every time you feel emotional, or you sense a high emotional state in others, think about what you are feeling and how best to manage those feelings to help yourself and others reach a positive outcome to the issue. It's the thinking that positively contributes to one's Emotional Intelligence. It's important to know how you process all the emotional information you absorb each day because it's in that processing that you can better asses your EI.

There are all sorts of tests that say they measure your Emotional Intelligence, but if your perception of self is somewhat skewed, isn't the information just more of the same? Most of us can't trust ourselves to be honest when it comes to evaluating our EI, so how valuable are any of these tests? If you're reading this book, you probably either sense that you need help with your emotions, or you have a desire to learn how to become more emotionally intelligent when it comes to making decisions. Either way, it doesn't matter. You've already taken the first step—you're thinking about the emotions you and others are feeling—you've worked through Step #1!

Chapter 2: Step #2—Creating Emotional Awareness

Since our childhoods, most of us have been taught to categorize and judge our emotions and the emotions of others. What is omitted in our early training is how to be more aware of our emotions and how they affect our decisions, behaviors, and beliefs about ourselves and others. For example, you may have learned as a child that crying was bad. Consequently, as an adult, you rarely cry and especially not in public. If someone you trusted had taught you that crying was only a way your body allows you to let off some built-up steam and stress, then perhaps you would be more capable of handling your own tears and feel more comfortable around others when they feel the need to cry.

That's the first step in creating more emotional awareness. Let go of your past judgments and categories where you have conveniently tucked away the emotions with which you feel uncomfortable. When you have tears or see someone else tearing up, grab a tissue and experience the waterworks. You'll be surprised at how refreshed you will feel when you let yourself experience the honesty of your emotions without the need to try to explain or rectify the situation. Just feel the raw emotion. As you think about what you are feeling with the tears, most of them will probably just dry up on their own, and you'll be consumed with wonder about the feelings associated with the tears.

There's No Right or Wrong Time to Feel Emotions

The process of awareness is enhanced when you close the door on judgment and criticism. Keep in mind; there's not a right or wrong time to feel your emotions. The only thing that is wrong is deciding not to feel at all. When you allow yourself to feel and think about the emotions you are feeling; you have increased awareness of how to use your feelings to positively impact your life.

Emotional awareness also reveals patterns in behaviors and thoughts that help you to identify and link similar emotions to events that may be triggers for you. When you are aware of emotional patterns in yourself and others, you can teach yourself to use this emotional information in your relationships, decision-making, and know when you are reacting irrationally to a situation. Then, instead of experiencing the typical "knee jerk" actions that may have challenged you in the past, you'll know to pause and give yourself a bit more time to think things through. You'll use your emotions in a more logical manner.

Learn to Listen and Observe

While awareness is necessary, it's not the end-all to gaining more Emotional Intelligence. Okay, so you're aware that every time you sit down at your desk at work, you feel a knot in your stomach. So, what? If you have identified the feeling but haven't given yourself time to think about why you feel this way, then there's no hope of resolving the underlying issues.

Listening and observing your body's reaction to emotions enhances your awareness and increases the likelihood that you'll seek a remedy for the discomfort. What must you do to dissolve the knot in your stomach? Well, if your feelings are telling you that you don't like your job, then it may be time to choose another company or perhaps a different career path. If you break out in a sweat every time you give a presentation, maybe you need more practice to increase your confidence. Some emotions cannot be avoided or ignored, but when you are aware of their influence, you can take steps to manage them better. That's practicing higher Emotional Intelligence.

As you become more aware of your emotions, you'll want to ask yourself some questions during the "think through" process. Some of the questions that are helpful are as follows.

- How are these feelings contributing to my setbacks or successes?
- Am I unduly distracted by these feelings or emotions?
- How am I being challenged by these emotions to allow myself to move forward in a more positive manner?
- What will enhance my ability to manage these emotions and use them to create stronger personal and professional relationships?

- What positive responses and behaviors do I see from others who might be experiencing similar emotions?

As you learn to listen and observe yourself and others' outward display of their feelings, use the time to reflect on the emotions you are witnessing. Think about how you would have handled the emotional situation. Give yourself time to consider alternative behaviors. Suddenly your Emotional Intelligence has changed from being an "inside" thought process to an external action that causes you to behave differently in future situations. You've successfully linked your previous thoughts to future outcomes, making it easier to predict favorable results. Greater Emotional Intelligence is an amazing thing, don't you think?

Breaking the Habits of Low Emotional Intelligence

Having low Emotional Intelligence is habit forming. You've become accustomed to ignoring yours and others emotions and so it's easier to continue to do what you've always done—turn away and distract yourself with other things. If you give emotions any thought at all, it's usually to pass quick judgment and then busy yourself with another activity. This can be a habit that is challenging to break.

There are two common habits that those with low Emotional Intelligence frequently practice. They are either easily offended, or they easily offend. Either way, these two habits block your ability to become more emotionally aware and use your emotions to benefit yourself and others. Pay attention to your thoughts when you witness the emotions of others. Do you say to yourself, "Oh for heaven sake—suck it up?" If so, learn to reprogram your self-talk. Start by thinking to yourself, "I wonder what is causing them to feel this way? What can I do to help?" This is called empathy or putting yourself in another's shoes so that you can open new avenues of understanding. If you get your feelings hurt at the drop of a hat, take notice of your feelings. Ask yourself, "Did I do something wrong? What can I do next time to improve my response to this type of situation?"

Deriding yourself for your feelings doesn't work, and it does nothing to help you break either of these two habits that inhibit greater Emotional Intelligence. There is a message in every emotion, so you must search for the message. What are your feelings telling you? How will being more aware of these feelings in the future help you to change your behaviors and improve your relationships? Now you've established new habits, making it much easier to eliminate the old ones.

Learning to Hear Your Emotions

Once your awareness has increased, you'll notice that emotions can be quite apparent in your voice as well as your body. Many people who are feeling fearful or are experiencing a lack of confidence will get a shaky voice. Of course, anger will make your voice increase in volume and speed. Frustration, on the other hand, often raises your voice a few octaves. Sorrow or disillusionment usually lowers your pitch and volume. When someone is attempting to control their emotions, their voice can become slower, more stilted and pronounced.

Couple the voice with body language, and you'll soon be reading a whole novel of emotions in others as well as yourself. For example, if someone is holding their body rather stiffly and their rate of speech is slower with their words pronounced more distinctly, you can almost bet they are feeling some strong emotions—usually anger or frustration. When you have successfully read the emotions lurking just beneath the surface of your conversation, you can act accordingly to defuse the emotion. Take a deep breath, accept that there is something wrong, and then take the appropriate action. What a transformation. Now you've used your Emotional Intelligence to set a higher standard of behavior than you would have previously exhibited.

Getting Comfortable with Your Emotions

Did you ever think that you'd be using the words comfort and emotions in the same sentence? If you're not quite a believer yet, that you can become comfortable with your feelings and emotions, keep practicing. Like anything else, the more you allow yourself to think and experience your emotions, and the more empathy you have for others, the easier Emotional Intelligence becomes.

At first when you have increased your emotional awareness, expect a flood of emotions to come streaming through your previously damned-up wall. Not to worry! Take one emotion and feeling at a time and give yourself time to think about it—identify it—manage it. Then you'll be ready for the next one and the next one until you've managed to work through an entire parade of emotions. It also takes some energy, so be patient with yourself. Enhancing your Emotional Intelligence takes effort, and allowing yourself to fully feel your emotions for the first time can be a bit draining. Trust me; it'll get better.

Once you get comfortable with your emotions, it will be much easier to deal with the emotions of others. Empathetic understanding will be second nature to you, and you'll earn the respect and admiration of others who may have previously been out of reach. People are attracted to those with high Emotional Intelligence, even those who pride themselves on being quite logical minded. Everybody likes to be heard, understood, valued and appreciated. That's what Emotionally Intelligent people do, and that's why others seek to have what they recognize in Emotionally Intelligent people.

Very little else sets you apart more than your Emotional Intelligence. It is as powerful and persuasive as having an extremely high IQ. In fact, studies show that Emotional Intelligence is more likely to bring success and well-being than those with high IQs. The Center for Creative Leadership (CCL) studied why seemingly intelligent corporate leaders found their careers stalled when their abilities and skills should have dictated otherwise. After a study of more than 20,000 individuals in 2,000 organizations what they discovered was that there were three main reasons for this phenomenon—all related to Emotional Intelligence.

1.   They had challenges handling change.

2.   They found it difficult to work as a team.

3.   They were incapable of developing strong working relationships.

Many CEOs have been relieved of their positions, not because of their lack of competence, but because of a lack of Emotional Intelligence. Furthermore, studies done by the Carnegie Institute of Technology showed that 85% of our success financially was due to how well we had learned to communicate, negotiate, and perform skills that required an awareness and understanding of others feelings and emotions. Just 15% of our financial success was due to our technical expertise and abilities.

Now that you're becoming more aware of the need to address your emotions and allow yourself to feel, let's look in the next chapter how you can move from chaos to control.

Chapter 3: Step #3—Moving from Chaos to Control

People of high Emotional Intelligence experience just as much chaotic emotions as the next person, the difference is they have learned how to control the chaos of emotions that others let run amuck. They are aware of their emotions and feelings, but instead of burying them, they take a breath and examine their feelings to determine how best to manage the emotions in a positive and constructive way. Sure, they feel all the emotions with the exception that they don't react impulsively and let their emotions create chaos. They practice self-control.

The truth is, as humans we experience the emotions before we have time to think about why we feel as we do. Those with a high degree of Emotional Intelligence give themselves permission not to have all the answers, to search for another alternative to the problem that would be more positive and productive. Emotional Intelligence requires that we take a moment to analyze how the emotions we are feeling will influence the outcome of the situation and impact us and those around us. Emotionally Intelligent people are confident enough to give the issue some time to simmer—time for them to contemplate different perspectives.

Exercise C.O.N.T.R.O.L.

Let me share with you what I mean by C.O.N.T.R.O.L.

C = Consider the Consequences

What will be the result of your actions? If you react without thinking about the consequences, your choices may not provide you with the desired outcome.

O = Optimism

Practicing optimism allows you to get in front of the emotion with positive thinking, even a little humor if necessary. People with positive outlooks almost always get more positive results from the decisions they make.

N = Neutralize the Emotions

Thinking about emotions neutralizes their power and calms the feelings. Most extreme emotions carry quite a punch, so when you can take the power out of the punch, your emotional state calms down, and you can think more rationally.

T = Take Ten

Take ten seconds to pause and consider the what and why of your feelings. This brief little pause along with a few deep breaths will position you to think calmly and make all-around better choices.

R = Regulate

Regulate your reactions in emotional situations. Apply all the elements of control, and help yourself and others to move away from the chaos of emotionally charged situations.

O = Openly Accept

Openly accept that you are going to experience emotionally charged situations. It's how you respond in these circumstances that will enhance your Emotional Intelligence. Be open to doing things differently, to accepting your own and others' emotions, to a willingness to admit your mistakes and hold yourself accountable for the decisions you make.

L = Look for Alternatives

Look for alternative behaviors, actions, and solutions to problems rather than giving into the chaotic emotions that have ruled you in the past. When you reach a higher degree of Emotional Intelligence, the alternatives will present themselves more clearly, and you'll be much more open to trying something different.

How Do You Get Control?

Good question! You get to control one moment at a time—one emotion at a time—one action at a time. As difficult as it might seem, there are some definite steps you can take to move from chaos to control.

1. Assume responsibility for your emotions and actions.

- Here's that word "consequences" again, but you must learn to accept the consequences of your actions. Hold yourself accountable. Admit you've made mistakes so that you can correct those things next time.

- Stop blaming others for your circumstances or dicey situations. Nobody should have the power to control your success but you. If you think they do, then you've given away too much of yourself—you've lost your inner strength and confidence.

- Put yourself in an emotional place that enables you to earn the respect of others. It's an incredible boost to know that others look up to you, that they depend on you to help them grow emotionally.

2.   Know what's most important to you.

- What do you value? What do you believe? What are you absolutely not willing to compromise?

- Know what you believe to be morally right, and then refuse to cross that line.

- What is your ethics? Do the decisions you make reflect high morals and ethical behavior?

3.   Reap all the benefits of calmness.

- Pay attention to your emotions. Know what creates stress in your life, then decide how you plan to remove the stress. Take action to come to calm.

- Stop the negative self-talk. If it takes writing down all your negative talk on a piece of paper to enable you to visualize the influence negative emotions have over your well-being, then write them down, rip them up, and dump them in the circular file.

- Practice deep breathing. Get some physical exercise. Do whatever it takes to spend some of that emotional energy. Then enjoy the calm.

You'll know you've reached greater levels of Emotional Intelligence when the decisions you make are rarely rushed or filled with emotional baggage. When your self-talk is positive, and you stop judging and stereotyping others, that's a clear indication that your Emotional Intelligence is gaining ground. When people are drawn to you and share their situations with you in hopes of guidance, then you'll know you've made great strides in improving your Emotional Intelligence.

Some people are born more intuitive, and feeling than others and some learn to have greater Emotional Intelligence at an early age, but no matter how old you are and what your position in life is, you can strengthen your ability to control and manage your emotions. There is nothing that is so permanent that it cannot be changed even if it's just by a little here and there. Perhaps the situation cannot be changed, but you can modify the way you perceive it, the way you plan to handle it. On the other hand, if there is something that happens that you feel changes everything, there are ways to face that battle as well. Those with high Emotional Intelligence see possibilities when others see problems; they see opportunities when others see obstacles. The choice is yours. So, what's it going to be? Well, it depends on your Emotional Intelligence, which provides you with great motivation to improve your EI.

I've heard it said that the greatest predictor of future outcomes is past behaviors; however, I'm not so sure that's true. I believe the more accurate predictor of future outcomes is the level of your Emotional Intelligence. Are you willing to look at your emotions in the eye and say to yourself, what can I do differently today that will give me better results than I had yesterday? How can I use the emotions and feelings I am having to influence my life's outcomes and bring me greater success? The choices you make and the actions you take as a result of these questions are truly life altering. Improving your Emotional Intelligence is what will be the best predictor of your future success.

Satisfaction in both your personal and professional life is more linked to Emotional Intelligence than almost anything else. More so than riches, IQ, or great careers, you'll find that Emotional Intelligence isn't too far behind the scenes of successful people. Our most memorable moments are teaming with individuals who have a high level of Emotional Intelligence. Think about when you felt the most loved, appreciated, valued, cherished, and needed, and then reflect on those who surrounded you in those moments. I'll bet you can identify many who had a high degree of Emotional Intelligence, right?

The Best Way to Control Yourself is to Help Others

Few things create more desire to perform at your peak, to reach heightened self-awareness, or to share the most love as others in your life who are willing to give the same back to you. Whether you have high Emotional Intelligence or yours is rather lacking at the moment, the people you find most attractive are usually those with high Emotional Intelligence. They somehow have the ability to draw people to them like wanderers to a warm fire on a cold winter's night.

We recognize Emotional Intelligence in others and want that for ourselves. You may not know what to call it, but you know there's something different about them that makes you enjoy their company. To examine your emotions and apply control over what might have been a turbulent past, observe and listen to those whom you recognize to have Emotional Intelligence. Watch how they monitor their emotions and express their feelings. Listen to how they encourage others to do the same. Do they take a little time to think things through before trying to resolve a problem? Do they value what others contribute in a meeting or a personal relationship? Then ask yourself how! How do they do what they do? Better yet, ask them to share their feelings with you. Emotionally Intelligent people don't mind opening up about their feelings. In fact, they usually welcome the opportunity.

Looking at the World through a Positive Lens

There was once two young men who were twins with entirely different outlooks on life. Although they had been raised by the same parents, in the same neighborhood, under the same economic situation, their futures reflected two completely different outlooks on the world. When asked why the one twin left home at such an early age and turned to using drugs, he responded, "Well, it was because of my parents and the neighborhood in which I lived." When asked why the other twin went on to college and became a successful businessman, he replied, "Well, it was because of my parents and the neighborhood in which I lived."

Each twin was raised in the same environment under the same circumstances, but with obviously different degrees of Emotional Intelligence. Each chose how they felt about their life's circumstances and how those feelings would influence the decisions they made in their lives. They even experienced the same emotions. What was different was how they chose to think about and control those emotions that set each twin's life path.

So, let me ask you—what will you choose? Will you choose chaos or control? Then ask yourself, what influence will these choices have over the rest of your life?

Chapter 4: Step #4—Redirecting Your Focus

What you choose to focus on is one of the most critical elements to being able to manage your emotions effectively. Whatever emotion you are focusing on at the time, you are actually feeding it, making it more powerful, and giving it enduring strength. By focusing on the negative feelings in your life, you not only strengthen them, but you weaken the positives. What you feed becomes stronger; what you starve gets weaker. Your emotions are rarely stagnating; they are either growing stronger or becoming weaker. The main part of the word "emotion" is "motion."

Your body feels the emotion before your mind comprehends its intensity or purpose. To prove my point, try a little experiment. Turn the corners of your mouth in a smile and begin to chuckle. Now strengthen that chuckle into full-blown laughter. It won't take long before your mind begins remembering something that gave you a giggle, and in just a matter of minutes, the positive is set into motion. Admit it; you weren't necessarily thinking about a happy moment before you began to laugh, right? As you focused on the real laughter, your thoughts followed with a happy memory.

The same can be said for clapping your hands and singing a happy tune. There's something about clapping your hands that won't allow you to feel depressed. Focus on the motion of clapping and the happy words to the song, and soon your outlook will be happy. It's like putting the positive in motion. Whatever feeling you focus on and feed becomes stronger. You don't necessarily have to be right in the middle of a positive experience to feel positive emotions; you just need to engage your mind and decide to be happy and remember something that makes you smile.

Have you ever had a shared story or joke with a family member or best friend and every time you begin to talk about it around others you just can't control your laughter? Because many in the group didn't experience the same event you did, they might not get the humor in the story, but it doesn't really matter because you and your friend are both so into the memory you turn into dribbling idiots and end up needing a tissue to wipe away the tears of laughter.

I shared one of these memories with my mother about a time my father wanted to go swimming but didn't have a suit. So, Mom and I went to the store and purchased a one-size-fits-all canary yellow swimsuit for him. What we discovered was that the clerk wasn't exactly truthful about the one-size-fits-all thing. After 30 minutes of desperate pulling and stretching, with a myriad of loud grunts and groans, my father exited the bathroom with a suit that showed every vulgar bump and wrinkles imaginable. With each step, the suit began to roll and creep down until he then resembled the Norge refrigerator repairman with his exposure getting more critically dangerous by the moment.

Oh, and I forgot to mention that my x mother-in-law was also witness to this bizarre event, and the expression on her face was that of shock and awe. To this day, I cannot share this story, especially in the presence of my mother, without doubling over with laughter. In fact, even seeing a one-size-fits-all sign in a clothing store is enough to set us off.

My point in telling this story is that you can decide to experience whatever emotion you focus on at the time. When I want to alleviate stress or depression, I often dredge up the memory of dad's most unflattering swim attire. If I really want to cement the feeling, I pick up the phone and call Mom, and we sputter on the phone for half an hour about the incident. If you want to magnify your focus on a feeling, share it in a story with others.

In Tony Robbins' book "Awaken the Giant Within," he presents the idea that the only reason people are motivated to do anything is to change the way they feel. They want to feel powerful, so they purchase a luxury car or a big house. They want to feel beautiful, so they lose weight or buy an expensive suit or dress. What many people fail to realize is that you can feel those emotions right now. Just decide to feel. You are already powerful and beautiful; you don't have to wait for something to happen to create those feelings. It's an amazing thing, but you can feel all those things with nothing changing in your life except your perspective.

If you want to feel like a giving person, give. If you want to be perceived as powerful, act powerfully. Not long ago, there was a young man who conducted an experiment. He hired a bunch of people to follow him through the streets of New York City with camera crews and act like an enthusiastic entourage. Thinking he must be a celebrity, complete strangers approached him on the street and began asking for his autograph. Viola, he was a star because he acted like a star.

Another example of creating emotions was when a man stood before marathon runners wearing a t-shirt that said "Free Hugs." People were approaching the end of the marathon and were worn out from the experience. They visibly wore the look of exhaustion on their faces and bodies. As they crossed the line almost ready to collapse, the young gentleman approached them with his arms held out and a huge smile on his face, ready to celebrate their efforts with a free hug. Their physical transformation was stunning. After they had got over the initial confusion, they shared the young man's big smile, held out their arms to welcome the hug, and shared a warm embrace that was both fun and energizing. Suddenly, their focus was on the hug of celebration instead of their aching bodies. Their focus was on the accomplishment instead of sore muscles and tired feet.

Let your body lead the way to open your mind's focus on all the possibilities of achieving greater Emotional Intelligence. Redirect your focus and let it lead the way to create Emotional Intelligence. Instead of burying your feelings, celebrate them, use them to push you to maximum performance, more meaningful relationships, and greater satisfaction in life. If it's up to you to forge your own path, why not make it a positive experience by focusing on all that is right and good. It doesn't mean that you will never feel the negatives, but they won't be strong enough to take control of your destiny.

Make Slaves of Your Negative Emotions

Just like you can use your positive feelings and emotions, you can also learn to use the negative emotions when they arise. For example, if you are aware of your negative emotions and recognize their patterns, then use them to improve yourself. Like that knot in your stomach, we discussed earlier that happened whenever you sat down at your desk at work, use it to motivate you to get another job or change your career to one that is more pleasing.

It takes courage to make slaves of your negative emotions. Why? Because negatives can be strong motivators for change, and change rarely happens without some struggle. Once you have a clear grasp on your feelings and understand how they can influence your life, you'll be willing to go through a time of discomfort to get to a better place. Suddenly, the tables will turn. Instead of being a slave to your negative emotions, you make them slaves to your actions and behaviors. Use them to push you to excellence.

First, you need to focus on the emotion, then on how you need to change your perspective, and lastly on your desired outcome. If you let the negative emotions control you, your focus will be limited and stifled. Remember, what you focus on becomes stronger, and everything you focus on is your choice. It's quite a freeing notion, this whole focus idea, wouldn't you say? If you want to wallow in self-pity, it's your choice. If you want to enjoy the positive feelings of a higher level of Emotional Intelligence, that's your choice as well.

Improving Your Ability to Focus

Remember the story of that marathon runner? When you are exhausted, your inability to focus will be evident in the choices and decisions you make. To improve your focus, get lots of sleep. It's difficult to feel positive when you're getting only a few hours of interrupted sleep each night. Your mind becomes foggy, and you begin to question every decision.

Next, eat properly. If your body is the first to indicate your feelings, then make sure it's strong. Eat healthy food that feeds the mind and muscles. Avoid overeating and creating a sluggish system that can barely focus on getting out of bed in the morning. There are certain foods that fuel thought—eat more of those. I can tell you; they usually don't come prepackaged or in the form of frozen dinners or salty snacks.

Get plenty of exercise to burn off the unwanted negative emotions and encourage you to focus on a healthier lifestyle. It's much easier to feel positive emotions when you know you're looking your best. Exercise and healthy food create "feel good" reactions in the mind and body. Being physically fit released chemicals and endorphins that expand your thinking and encourage better focus and greater cognitive thought.

Whatever you do, do it now. Don't wait until you look better, feel better, have achieved more success in your job, or have found that one-in-a-million relationship. Remember, it's a decision, so decide now to focus on feeling positive and rejuvenated. Focus on where you want to be instead of where you are. Focus on what will happen when you achieve Emotional Intelligence.

Chapter 5: Step #5—Practicing a Daily Dose of Emotional Intelligence

We're such an instant society, always so busy running here and there that we rarely take the time to simply sit and reflect upon our feelings. In fact, just reading it might make some feel like they've returned to the '70s era where people walked the streets passing out flowers and sitting on the curb chanting. Who knows, perhaps that was the beginning of us thinking about Emotional Intelligence, and we lost touch with our feelings somewhere along the way.

As much as I believe Emotional Intelligence plays a significant role in all our lives, I too let my busy life get in the way of taking a few moments out of each day to focus on my feelings. Most people's lives are consumed by family, friends, careers, financial worries, and just everyday stuff that gets in the way of taking a little time for ourselves. At the end of a busy day, all we can think about is unplugging and turning into mindless little television zombies. The only emotions we want to reflect on at the end of the day is how we're going to address our exhaustion.

Well, here's a thought. What if that exhaustion is caused by your inability to take time for yourself? What if your day flowed much smoother and your energies were revived because you gave yourself a daily dose of Emotional Intelligence? You'd be amazed at how a few minutes escape each morning and afternoon would make such a difference in your energy level. Unresolved or misunderstood emotions can take their toll on your energy level.

There are three ways to deal with your feelings. Some people are clueless when it comes to understanding their emotions. They don't deal with their feelings because they refuse to consider the fact that they even have any emotions. Instead, they plow through life telling themselves they're loners, that they feel entirely comfortable being alone. Then, there are those people who are aware they have emotions and feelings that sometimes may be getting in the way of their relationships, but they don't know what to do with them. Instead of discovering how to deal with their emotions, they push them aside and make weak promises that things will get better when they are more financially stable, or when they lose weight or when they get a better job or a nicer car. What they don't realize is that their low Emotional Intelligence is what could be keeping them from greater achievement. If you've been putting off dealing with your emotions until tomorrow, consider this, tomorrow never comes. You're always in today—today is the time to practice Emotional Intelligence.

Then there are the ones, maybe just like you, who are seeking to improve your Emotional Intelligence by learning how to practice empathy, understanding, and awareness of yours and others' emotions. Stop reacting every time you have an emotional crisis, and start responding by giving your emotions some further thought. That's the difference between reacting and responding. When you respond to an emotional situation, you have already given it some thought. You have compared the feelings you are now having to others you have had in the past. You had already asked yourself when you experienced similar feelings how you planned to handle them in the future. Now, the future is here, and you are better prepared for the successful management of your emotions. You have just increased your Emotional Intelligence.

Practice Makes More Perfect Practice

It's important to understand that increasing your Emotional Intelligence is a lifelong endeavor. It's not something you "get" today, wipe your brow and let out a sigh of relief that you have finally reached your peak. Emotional Intelligence is a mountain or understanding and awareness that has no peak. You will never reach the top; however, each day brings you new vistas of serenity and calm experiences that clear your vision and prepare you for your next climb.

This is a tough one for those who pride themselves on perfection because you will never reach the perfect level of Emotional Intelligence. What is possible is that each day you think about your feelings and allow yourself to contemplate how you will do things differently next time, then place yourself in social and professional environments that enable you to practice dealing with yours and others emotions; you gain ground. If it helps you, think of Emotional Intelligence as being a mountain with many lookout points, and you get to see a whole new, panoramic view every day.

Talking about practicing Emotional Intelligence isn't enough; now it's time for some sound practice. First, practice on yourself. Once you've given some thought to your feelings, to why you reacted a certain way in an emotionally charged situation, then step out and practice your Emotional Intelligence on others. Observe the facial expressions and body language of a group you are in, and when someone seems stressed question them further about what is causing their hurt or pain. It could be they are on an emotional high, and that's a good time to ask them to share their experience as well. Celebrate their happy event with them. Enjoy their success or experience, their joy, and laughter. Emotions aren't always bad, you know. Some are over-the-top fantastic, and you can now share those feelings while you practice your Emotional Intelligence.

Creating a Safe Environment

If practicing your Emotional Intelligence is going to be a complete turn-around for you, make sure you create a safe environment. Begin practicing with people you trust. You may even share with them how you are feeling, that's a wonderful way to practice. Choose individuals who care about you and want to see you succeed. A word of warning, these may not be your bar buddies or your co-workers. If you are going to explore your feelings and share your goals with another, make sure it is someone with high Emotional Intelligence. They will be the ones who will show you empathy and understanding, and you will be able to learn from them how to handle your emotions.

It can be difficult to trust your emotions when you've never even admitted you have any, or when you've prided yourself on not showing them. So, when you first come out, so to speak, do so with people who are not emotionally starved or isolated from their feelings. Once you have thought about your feelings, you'll need to trust them so that you can be encouraged to step outside your routine and show empathy to yourself and others.

You're on the precipice of change, and change requires things of you that might be difficult and challenging. Keep at it; the payoff is incredible. Once you experience successful strides in building your Emotional Intelligence, you'll never want to go back to that person you were yesterday who felt something was missing. There will be a void that finally begins to close, and a completeness within yourself that you've never had before.

That's one advantage of transformation; you can look back and see how far you've come; enjoy the journey. Others who have always had a high degree of Emotional Intelligence might never appreciate what they have quite as much as those who have to work hard to get it. What takes more work to accomplish is usually appreciated more than what comes naturally or easily. You've worked hard and earned your success, and that's a plus in my book.

Expect the Unexpected

What will begin to happen will be just short of miraculous. If you have been a loner in the past, and you start to gain ground with your Emotional Intelligence, you'll soon find yourself attracting friends, and people that you previously felt were out of your league. If you felt trapped in a "go nowhere" job, you'll be more willing to take a risk and step out to search for something that is more suitable to your newly gained Emotional Intelligence. In fact, you may have people come to you wanting you to join their team. The more Emotional Intelligence you get, the more you understand and empathize with yourself and others, the more you'll change into that person you always wanted to become.

Reaching greater heights of Emotional Intelligence is directly proportionate to how much you practice empathizing and understanding yours and others feelings. Practice a little and gain a little ground each day. Practice a lot, and you grow by leaps and bounds. It's all about choice, and the choice is yours. You set your limits and boundaries.

When you build your Emotional Intelligence, you will experience the most unexpected occurrences. People will begin asking for your opinion, and "surprise—surprise," you'll look forward to sharing your ideas and feelings. You may become the "go to" guy in office meetings. You might get brave and introduce yourself to an attractive stranger at a party, and he or she welcomes the intrusion with open arms and enticing conversation. You might be able to save the rocky relationship you are currently in, returning to your first feelings of love and admiration. Emotional Intelligence brings more surprises than you can imagine, so take a deep breath and get ready for the ride of your life.

Chapter 6: Step #6—Predicting & Preventing Outcomes

In every aspect of our lives, it has been studied and proven that those with higher Emotional Intelligence can predict more positive outcomes in their personal and professional endeavors. Let's examine the influence of Emotional Intelligence from early adolescence to adulthood.

Predicting Academic Success

When children move into puberty, their hormones spur on the whole gamut of emotional experiences. To say that these emotions and feelings can be somewhat distracting is an understatement. If you begin to develop Emotional Intelligence at an early age, you are better prepared to manage these emotions and focus on academics successfully. Students who have a high Emotional Intelligence are calmer, more satisfied with their social networks, feel more supported by their family and friends, and can successfully handle the anxiety that comes with test taking and peer pressure.

Because early positive perceptions and beliefs about yourself are the most important elements in the development into stable adulthood, those who learn Emotional Intelligence in their youth are more likely to continue to gain more EI as they mature. Emotional Intelligence positions them for future management and leadership roles as they enter the workplace.

Influence of EI on Your Health and Well-being

Doctors Schutte and Malouff, researchers in the area of Emotional Intelligence conducted a study in 2007, where they researched the correlation between Emotional Intelligence and physical health. What they found was that people with high Emotional Intelligence made better decisions and were less likely to use alcohol, drugs, and food as a way to self-medicate and handle unresolved emotional issues. Continual unresolved emotional issues cause a great deal of physical and mental stress, which can take its toll on your overall health. Learn how to address your feelings and emotions, and your physical health gets a giant boost. The less stress you feel, the more you can focus on the positive goals you want to achieve.

Developing More Complex Relationships

What has been developed, whether low or high Emotional Intelligence, in school, will be a good indication of what to expect as you begin to seek more complex personal and professional relationships. Those with higher Emotional Intelligence are more likely to build secure, stable, and more satisfying interpersonal relationships, says a study by Yale professors Mayer and Salovey, in 1999 study.

It stands to reason, that when you have a high Emotional Intelligence, you are more able to avoid arguments and fights with your significant other. Your outlook on life is more positive, and you are in touch with yours and your partner's feelings. Most people with high Emotional Intelligence are less aggressive and have a calm, peaceful manner, which is much more conducive to a long-term, rewarding relationship.

Emotional Intelligence in the Workplace

Emotionally Intelligent people tend to make better choices when they decide on a career path, so they avoid much of the job-hopping and career changes that plague others whose decisions are impaired by emotions and feelings of which they are unaware. The benefit to making positive initial choices is that they experience greater job satisfaction and have more years to climb that ladder of success and to grow into a leadership role that brings with it more power and financial gain.

People enjoy being close to those with high Emotional Intelligence; therefore, they receive greater peer support and higher supervisor reviews. This also brings with it more pay increases and higher commissions. Salespeople with high Emotional Intelligence usually experience less rejection and more sales because they sell with empathy and understanding. It's a proven fact that people buy from those they like, and people like those with high Emotional Intelligence. There is also less burnout experienced by people with high Emotional Intelligence. Their energy levels are higher and they are more positive about their position in life, so there is less complaining and exhaustion at the end of their workday.

Emotionally Intelligent Leaders

Professors Freshman and Rubino, who was also Director of the Health Administration Program at California State University, held a study in 2002, showing that high Emotional Intelligence is a critical component of those in management and leadership roles. They discovered that people with high Emotional Intelligence experienced less turnover in the workplace and benefited from more productivity. When workers are not distracted or discouraged by overbearing and unsupportive leaders, they are much more positive and productive.

Here are a few examples of companies that have significantly benefited by incorporating Emotional Intelligence into their corporate structure.

- Sheraton—when Sheraton decided to include an Emotional Intelligence program, guess what happened? Their market share climbed by a whopping 24 percent.

- Pepsi—as Pepsi began to study the results of executives with high Emotional Intelligence, what they found was that their productivity was 10% greater than those with low Emotional Intelligence. They also discovered that they benefited from 87% less turnover. To put these figures into dollar amounts, what this meant to the Pepsi Corporation was an incredible 3.75 million in value and a 1,000% increase in their return on investment.

- Loreal—Loreal was another company who stepped out to examine what all the fuss was about regarding this Emotional Intelligence thing. What they found when investigating their salespeople was that those with high Emotional Intelligence sold 2.5 million more than those with lower EI.

When managers and leaders focus on good communications and pay attention to and support the feelings of their people, these reported financial gains make perfect sense. Executives who not only pay attention to what is said but also to what is not said, are far ahead of the game. When they can clearly see the stress on the faces of their employees and read the body language of workers who may be suffering from overwork or a lack of recognition, they can remedy these situations before the emotions can negatively impact production.

Managers and leaders who proactively engage their employees instead of reactively trying to put out the fires can spend more time in visionary pursuits that maintain their executives and company position as the industry's top dogs. It's no accident that Pepsi and Loreal have been leaders in their respective industries for over a hundred years. It's by design; it's by incorporating the ideas of those with high Emotional Intelligence that have given them marketplace longevity.

Taking Preventative Measures

As much as high Emotional Intelligence can predict positive outcomes to people's future, it should also be the encouraging element for you to take preventative measures to ensure you experience greater success. If you have suffered setbacks in your relationships or career, isn't it great to know that you can now take preventative measures to put you on a more successful path? Taking just a few minutes from your day to practice thinking about your feelings and how you can apply Emotional Intelligence in your decision making is being proactive in taking preventative measures that can help you to have more positive outcomes.

If you want to be more productive, then deal with the emotions before they deal with you. Do a little preventative maintenance and be one minded. When it's time to think about your feelings, do that. Then, when it's time to work you can do that without being distracted by anger or frustration that interferes with your job.

Ten Way to Prevent Negative Outcomes

1. Speak your mind. Be honest with yourself about your emotions and feelings. Don't interrupt your self-talk with negative comments. Refuse to trivialize your feelings; they are real and they can be used to create more positive outcomes.

2. Live in the present. Stop worrying about yesterday, and give your feelings and emotions your full attention right now. The only time you should think about the past in when

making decisions on how to better handle your current feelings. If you practice Emotional Intelligence and you have poor results, give yourself time to improve. Don't quit!

3.   Find connections between past emotions and current feelings. How you feel about today is probably a result of what happened to you in the past. Allow yourself to make the connection so that you can prevent more adverse outcomes.

4.   Take thought breaks. Make a habit of taking breaks to think—just like some people take a coffee break. It will relax and rejuvenate your mind. You've heard that some executives take power naps. Why not take a thinking nap? Let your mind focus on your feelings and then find a solution to a pressing problem. Decide how to use your feelings to create more positive outcomes in your life.

5.   Let your body speak. Listen to what your body is trying to tell you. If you are getting frequent headaches and stomach aches, it might mean that it's time for you to use your Emotional Intelligence and deal with your feelings in a way that will relieve your body of having to do all the work.

6.   Clear your self-perceptions. If you aren't sure you are getting an accurate reading on yourself, ask a trusted friend to help you out with your self-analysis. Take an inventory of your perceptions. Ask a close friend how they perceive you. You might be surprised when you hear what is said.

7.   Emotions are powerful. Sometimes, if emotions are not properly dealt with, they express themselves in other ways. One of the ways is in our dreams. You may want to try recording your dreams. What are your dreams trying to tell you? Do you have a recurring dream that might have some significant meaning?

8.   Daily inventory. Take a daily inventory of your feelings. This is a good way to begin thinking about your emotions and gaining Emotional Intelligent. Ask yourself how you are feeling today? What is different about today than yesterday? What will be different about tomorrow than today? Doing this allows you to plan how you can create more positive future outcomes.

9.   Create a thought journal. If you are having trouble focusing on your feelings, write down your feelings in a reflection journal. There's something about writing that makes your mind slow down and focus.

10.   Don't dwell on the negatives. Concentrate on the feelings, not the adverse event or outcome. If the feelings are negative, deal with the feelings—not the event or result of those feelings.

If all this is a bit too touchy-feely for you, if you think that thinking about feelings sounds weak, then consider this. Scientists, professors, national speakers and authors, even presidents have used Emotional Intelligence to achieve greatness. There was nothing soft about their positions or methods of leadership. Those same leaders with high Emotional Intelligence have helped us treat severe mental illness, taught us physics and calculus, led their industries in production, written books that helped thousands of people reach peak performance, and led us through wars. You'll be in good company when you chose to use higher Emotional Intelligence.

Conclusion:

Thank you for purchasing *Emotional Intelligence: The Complete Step-by-Step Guide on Self-Awareness—Controlling Your Emotions and Improving Your EQ.* We've given you a lot to think about—most importantly, how you can use your Emotional Intelligence to achieve greater successes in your life. Practicing these six steps to success will help you build positive personal and professional relationships, make better decisions, and find greater satisfaction in your career choices. A new and exciting world of opportunity is about to open up to you as you gain Emotional Intelligence.

I hope we have helped to change your perceptions and to think about how to manage your emotions and feelings. Emotions can cripple you or empower you; the choice is yours. The steps you have learned in this book will help you as you journey through some of your unresolved feelings and emotions. If the reading of this book leaves you hungry for more information, you might want to read some of my other works. Check out *Emotional Intelligence: The Definitive Guide to Understanding Your Emotions, How to Improve Your EQ and Your Relationships*, and *Emotional Intelligence Mastery: How to Master Your Emotions, Improve Your EQ, and Massively Improve Your Relationships.*

Obviously, there is a recurring theme in these works, and that is my belief that emotions and feelings matter. Feelings are core to our most basic needs. Feelings drive us, motivate us, and inspire us to achieve. Emotions created by those feelings also have tremendous influence in our life's outcome. Emotions in themselves are not good or bad; it's how we deal with them that determines whether they have a positive or negative impact. The important thing for you to remember is that you are in the driver's seat. The feelings belong to you. Either you chose to control your emotions, or you chose to let them control you. What's it going to be?

We are all born with different degrees of Emotional Intelligence, just as we are born with different levels of IQ. Even though our Emotional Intelligence is inherent, it doesn't mean it cannot be increased and improved. That's what this book was all about, adopting ways to create high Emotional Intelligence. You are now victim to your knowledge. After reading this book, it will be most difficult for you to return to an emotionally devoid life. Having journeyed with me through the pages of this book, the most logical progression will be to put these six steps into action and follow these proven strategies to lead you to a greater empathy and understanding of yours and others emotions and feelings.

As you focus on your future of higher Emotional Intelligence, I look forward to hearing from you about all the positive outcomes you'll be experiencing. It will also be interesting to hear you share your feelings and emotions about all the unexpected things that will happen to you along the way. The growth won't be immediate and you'll have your share of challenges, but your increased Emotional Intelligence will help you to weather the storms that working through some of these emotions may create.

Don't wait to work on the steps presented in this book; do it today. As soon as you finish reading, set this book down and take a moment or two to reflect on your feelings. Ask yourself how you are feeling after having finished the book. Where do you expect this information to take you? What do you think will change when you begin to practice more Emotional Intelligence in your personal and professional life?

Don't be surprised when your friends and family members notice a real difference in your manner and outlook. Basque in the added attention you will receive when you put these steps to work for you and begin to make choices and decision based on sound emotions and feelings.

I hope you're ready to enjoy all the benefits of increasing your Emotional Intelligence, of becoming more aware of yours and others feelings, and reaping the rewards in store for you as you move through life with more empathy and understanding. Who knows, sharing your feelings might become so second nature to you that you'll want to share how you felt as you read these books and encourage others to read them as well.

Thank you for taking the time to read this book. If you believe it helped you to get in touch with your feelings and emotions, to gain more knowledge about how to improve your Emotional Intelligence, please take just a few more moments to post a review on amazon. It would be so appreciated, and you'd be in a position to help others raise their Emotional Intelligence as well.

Thank you once again, and congratulations on all the improved relationships, better decisions, and greater opportunities I know you will experience after having practiced these six steps to improve your Emotional Intelligence.

Book – II
Emotional Intelligence

21 Most Effective Tips and Tricks on Self-Awareness, Controlling Your Emotions, and Improving Your EQ

Introduction

Do you get stressed easily? Do you have difficulty asserting yourself and your needs? Do you often make assumptions? Do you do everything to assert that assumption? Do you hold a grudge? Do you get into a lot of arguments? Do you often feel misunderstood? Do you have a hard time understanding other people? Do you think that other people are just too sensitive? Do you refuse to listen to other people's point of view? Do you blame other people for your mistakes? If you answered yes to most of these questions, you may have low emotional intelligence.

People with emotional intelligence are not afraid of change. They are not afraid to ask tough questions. They are patient and yet persistent. They also easily develop relationships that are based on trust and respect. They are also able to resolve conflicts positively.

Today, it's not enough to have a high IQ to succeed, you need to have high emotional intelligence, too. According to leading psychologists, emotional intelligence affects performance. It has a huge impact on your professional success. A study conducted by TalentSmart shows that emotional intelligence or IE (popularly known as EQ) is the biggest predictor of job performance. That's because emotional intelligence is the foundation of all critical skills – empathy, anger management, assertiveness, flexibility, accountability, communication, presentation skills, and stress tolerance. Over ninety percent of the people who are doing well at work also have high emotional intelligence. A study also shows that people with high emotional intelligence earn more money. There's no job that does not require high emotional intelligence.

Hence, every individual should develop the mature emotional intelligence skills needed to better empathize, understand, and deal with other people.

The good news is that emotional intelligence is something that you could develop over time. This book contains practical and easy to follow steps that will help increase your emotional intelligence.

In this book, you'll learn:

What emotional intelligence is

Traits of people with high emotional intelligence

Traits of people with low emotional intelligence

21 practical tips that will help you increase your emotional intelligence

How to set personal boundaries

How to get to know yourself deeply

How to increase your optimism and resilience

Real stories of people with low and high emotional intelligence

30 empathy statements

100 techniques to help you beat stress

And more!

Emotional intelligence helps you make good life decisions – in a sense, it helps increase the quality of your life.

It's time to get out of the emotional roller coaster that you're in. This book will help you understand and manage your emotions. This book will help increase your self-control, conscientiousness, adaptability, motivation, and trustworthiness. Most of all, this book helps you understand other people more so that you can build deeper and more meaningful relationships

Thanks again for purchasing this book and I hope that you enjoy it.

The Truth About Emotional Intelligence

We all know what IQ is – it is the measurement of your intelligence. Having a high IQ is like having a high cognitive capital in the information economy. It helps you solve problems and learn things quickly. It also helps you overcome attention disorders. High IQ is associated with occupational status and success, perceptual abilities, emotional sensitivity, artistic preference, altruism, achievement motivation, linguistic abilities, and practical knowledge.

But, many experts say that having a high IQ is not enough. You also need to have high emotional intelligence to thrive in this modern world.

Emotional intelligence is often referred to as EI or EQ (emotional quotient). The term was popularized by Daniel Coleman in his 1995 book entitled *"Emotional Intelligence"*. Since then, the word "emotional intelligence" has become a buzzword amongst psychology and behavioral science experts.

EQ is defined as the ability to identify and understand our own emotions and those of others. Emotional intelligence is associated with important life skills such as self-management, social awareness, ability to beat stress, accountability, listening skills, open-mindedness, communication skills, trustworthiness, conscientiousness, self-motivation, and likeability.

To understand this definition better, let's take a look at the case of Jackie – a middle manager of a software development company. She's got a degree at Harvard University and she's exceptionally intelligent. She has a strong passion for coding and she can create and read codes in multiple languages.

She's driven and she has the ability to drive excellence. She definitely has high IQ. But, her life is out of balance. She's too obsessed with work that she compromises her relationships and health. She also lacks humility. She believes that she's the only one who can do it all so she micromanages her employees.

She doesn't listen to her employees and she dismisses ideas that are not her own. She also lacks empathy and has no accountability. When things go wrong, she looks for an escape goat – someone to blame for her mistakes and shortcomings. She's close-minded and she steals credits for completed tasks and projects. She bullies her employees into seeing things her way.

Because of this, she is unable to get the best from her people. She fires people at whim and often engage in a power struggle with her co-managers. When she's stressed, she lashes out on her team. The firm was sued for emotional torts such as intentional infliction of distress on employees, defamation, and abuse of process. Jackie's boss didn't have a choice but to let her go.

Jackie has low emotional intelligence. People with low intelligence are impatient and they often feel like other people don't get their point. They think that being liked at work is unnecessary and overrated. They do not understand how other people feel and they try to downplay other people's feelings. They have a hard time maintaining a good relationship and can't cope with negative emotions. They lack accountability and empathy. They have the tendency to trivialize emotions in general. They lack compassion and they like to play games.

Now, let's look at another person with low emotional intelligence – Christine. She's a computer programmer. She's generally a nice person to the point that she allows people to take advantage of her. She's unable to say no, so she spreads herself too thin. She also easily gets overwhelmed and stressed. She's also close-minded and not open to new ideas. She constantly interrupts other people and she has poor listening skills.

Although she's the goody-goody type, Christine is unable to forgive. Five years ago, his fiancé, Kurt, left her at the altar. It's been five long years, but Christine is still bitter. She's unable to establish new relationships. She's also prone to emotional breakdown when exposed to stressful situations. She's stuck in a job that she doesn't like for five years because she doesn't like change. She's afraid to try new things and step out of her comfort zone. She expects the worst in every situation.

Like Jackie, Christine has low emotional intelligence. People with low emotional intelligence are often pessimistic and they invalidate other people's joy. They often need rules to feel secure. They are rigid, inflexible, and afraid to try something new. They carry grudges and they are unforgiving. They often present themselves as a victim.

Now, take a look at Ann's story. Ann was born to a poor family. Her parents didn't have enough money to send her to college. So, Ann had to work at McDonald's to send herself to college. It was difficult, but she was persistent. She wanted to get out of poverty so she worked hard. After graduating from college, she was hired as a junior manager in a software development company.

Ann was well-liked because she listened to her subordinates. She let her team have time to rest. She was good at reading cues and body language. She used these skills to motivate and influence her team. Because of this, her software development team consistently did well and Ann was eventually promoted to vice president in just three years with the company.

Ann has the ability to identify her emotions. She knows when she's stressed so she uses healthy ways to reduce her stress – she runs, plays instruments, and writes in a journal. She also uses humor to deal with challenges and difficult situations. She has a good balance of work and recreation. She doesn't hold grudges and she deals with conflict in a calm manner. She puts herself in other people's shoes.

Because of this, she's well-liked at work. Ann is confident enough to know that she's good at her work. But, she's humble enough to know that she can't do it all. She knows when to delegate, but she doesn't simply pass the responsibility to her subordinates. She constantly checks on her people to make sure that they are well taken cared of.

People with high emotional intelligence are aware of their emotions. They know what makes them happy, sad, frustrated, stressed, and tired. Because of this, they are able to manage their emotions and respond to them accordingly.

Emotions are neither good or bad. But, they are either appropriate or inappropriate. They are also either negative or positive. Anger, for example, is a negative emotion, but getting angry is not necessarily a bad thing. Anger helps you identify your personal boundaries. It helps you point out the things that you are not willing to tolerate. But, lashing out at someone who tripped over your shoes is a bit inappropriate, to say the least.

Let's look at another emotion – happiness. It's a positive emotion. In its purest form, it is neither good or bad. It's just an emotion. But, if you feel happy when someone else fails, your happiness is definitely inappropriate.

Emotionally intelligent people express emotions that are appropriate to the situation. They are able to interpret and respond appropriately to their own emotions. They also have the ability to recognize and respond appropriately to other people's emotions.

People with high emotional intelligence are compassionate, but they are also assertive. They do not allow other people to walk all over them or disrespect their time. They are humble, but they are also aware of their value. They express their feelings clearly and directly. They also have the ability to balance emotions with reality, logic, and reason. They do not sweat over the small stuff and they definitely do not shout at waiters for bringing the wrong order. Negative emotions such as fear or anxiety do not cripple them.

Emotionally competent people are often optimistic, but also realistic. They are interested in other people's emotions. They are resilient and they stay strong even when faced with challenges and adversity.

According to Daniel Coleman, there are five key areas of emotional intelligence – self-awareness, motivation, self-regulation, empathy, and social skills.

Self-Awareness

We are always told to cultivate self-awareness. Sadly, not all of us are aware of who we are.

According to wise Chinese philosophers, self-awareness is the strongest weapon that you can use to defend yourself from your enemies. When you have a strong sense of who you are, it's difficult for other people to manipulate you.

Self-awareness is also linked to humility. When you have an accurate assessment of who you are, you'll know that the world does not revolve around you. When you are aware of who you are, it is easier to become who you want to be.

Self-awareness helps you live up to your full potential. It helps you exercise compassion and self-care.

Empathy

Empathy is the ability to put other people's shoes. It is the ability to understand other people's feelings and experiences. It helps you understand people better and it improves your cultural competence. It improves your leadership skills as it's a tool that you can use to motivate others.

Empathy is probably the most important skill that you can develop. It allows you to treat people the way they want you to treat them. It is important because it allows you to build meaningful relationships. It helps you deal with interpersonal conflict and helps reduce tensions.

Social Skills

Do you avoid speaking to others? Do you talk only about yourself? Do you often talk down to others? Do you lack patience? Do you find it hard to listen to others? Do you find it hard to compromise? Do you overthink other people's responses when you are in a social gathering? Do you find it hard to find common ground with most people? Are you unpopular? Do you say the wrong things all the time? Do you hate being around many people? Do you find it hard to understand social norms? Do you look at your phone when you're talking to someone?

If you answered yes to most of these questions, chances are, you lack social skills. Having great social skills helps you build meaningful relationships. It increases your efficiency because you don't have to avoid people you don't like so much. It allows you to establish a flourishing career.

People with high EQ are social butterflies, so they are generally likeable. They are patient. They are also open to new ideas. They smile when speaking to others. They are generally friendly and accommodating. They also listen before they speak.

Emotional Management

Do you often experience a nervous breakdown when exposed to extreme stress? Do you have persistent feelings of guilt? Do you have unreasonable fears? Do you have a hard time controlling your anger? If you have a hard time controlling negative emotions such as guilt, stress, fear, and anger, you definitely have low EQ.

But, how important is it to control your emotions? To illustrate the importance of emotional management, let's look at Walter's story, an electronic engineer. He is generally a good guy. He loves his family and he's a hard worker, too. But, Walter is also emotionally unstable. He's moody. He also has a tendency to get violent when he loses his temper. He gets angry over little things.

One day, his wife, Fern, took out Walter's toolbox and borrowed his hammer to do simple woodwork. But, she forgot to return it. After a long day at work, Walter found his hammer lying on the floor. Now, an emotionally stable person would just pick up the hammer and let this pass. But, Walter is an emotional mess. He got so angry that his hammer was not in the right place that he hit his wife over it. Devastated, Fern left Walter and took their two kids with her.

The ability to manage your emotions will help you handle conflicts in a healthier way. It increases your logical reasoning and inner peace. It also allows you to resist emotional manipulation. It helps you stay cool even when someone is pushing your buttons.

Let's take a look at the life of a lovely and emotionally stable woman, named Kylie, who works at an advertising firm. Her work is really cool and exciting. She consistently performed well and was up for promotion. This angered her more senior colleagues. Her co-workers tried to provoke her to derail her focus. They tried to make her feel worthless and unworthy by talking down to her and spreading rumors about her.

Fortunately, Kylie has high EQ. She is aware of her emotional triggers so it's easy for her to control her emotions when provoked. When her co-workers say off-handed remarks, she takes a deep breath and tries to ignore. She doesn't take these statements personally. She understands that these remarks are just a result of her colleagues' jealousy and limiting beliefs. She tries to walk away from things and situations that make her feel uncomfortable.

Self-motivation

It's hard to wake up in the morning when you're not motivated, you'll feel tired and depressed all the time. You'll have a hard time finishing your tasks and achieving your goal.

Let's take a look at the life of Karen, a student of medicine. She's brilliant and she wanted to be a doctor since she was a kid. She was determined to turn that dream into reality. But, something happened during her second year in med school. Her brother was diagnosed with a rare disease. The doctor could not do anything to save him. After six months of struggle, her brother died. It crushed Karen's heart. She didn't know where to go or what to do. Everything seemed bleak. She quit med school and worked as a medical transcriptor.

She does not perform well at her work. She always makes mistakes. She's passive and she constantly procrastinates. Many of her colleagues think that she's lazy. But, the truth is, she just lacks motivation.

If you seem stuck in life, you may lack self-motivation – the inner fire that fuels your desire for achievement. So, in a sense, it helps you win at life. It increases your personal satisfaction and helps you fulfill your potential.

All facets of emotional intelligence (social skills, self-awareness, self-regulation, self-motivation, and empathy) are equally important. To thrive in life, you need to have the ability to recognize your emotions and regulate them. You also need to increase your motivation to reach your full potential. And most of all, you must have empathy and social skills to build deep and meaningful relationships.

Emotional intelligence is the most powerful tool that you can use to handle the most uncomfortable situations. If you're a customer service representative, emotional intelligence helps you deal with difficult customers. If you're a soldier, you can use your EI or EQ to increase your mental strength amidst the chaos and violence around you. If you're a leader, EI helps you build relationships with your subordinates and create a unified culture of tolerance and optimism.

Whoever you are and whatever you do, you need to have high emotional intelligence to thrive and succeed in life.

Tip #1: Develop A Strong Sense of Who You Are

There's one person that we spend most of our days with - ourselves. Yet, it's an irony that most of us don't know ourselves very well.

To effectively manage your emotions, you must have a strong sense of who you are. You should have a clear understanding of your strengths, weaknesses, traits, likes, and dislikes. You must know what makes you tick and what makes you snap.

To know more about yourself, practice writing down everything that you know about yourself so far:

> *What kind of a person are you?*
>
> *What makes you sad?*
>
> *What makes you happy?*
>
> *Who makes you happy?*
>
> *Are you a cheerful person?*
>
> *What makes you leap out of bed?*
>
> *Do you like helping others?*

Knowing yourself does not only increase your emotional intelligence, it also allows you to make good life decisions. It keeps you from making bad decisions. It allows you to identify your passions and do the things that are important to you.

Self-awareness allows you to regulate your emotions. It increases resiliency – an invisible trait that allows you to bounce back whenever you get knocked down by challenges.

Funny girl Amy Poehler said, *"You attract the right things when you have a sense of who you are"*. You cannot achieve great things unless you know who you really are. Self-knowledge is also the starting point of self-improvement.

To illustrate this point, let's study the story of Edward - a young lawyer. He's a brilliant man, but he does not know who he is. Until now, he has no sense of who he is. He does things just to fit in.

He engages with people pleasing behavior. He is not aware of his values and what's important to him. Thus, he is unable to resist flattery and other forms of manipulation.

When he graduated from law school, he was hired as an associate in a big law firm. At that time, he did not know what his priorities were. He built a career protecting criminals. When he turned 60, he was rich and successful, but he felt empty. He did not know what he stood for, he wasn't able to find his purpose in life, and at his deathbed, all he got were regrets.

Self-awareness is one of the most valuable assets that you can have. It helps you play with your strengths and adapt to any situation. It also allows you to identify your weakness.

There are five building blocks that make up who you are – your values, interests, temperament, life mission, and personal strengths.

Values are defined as general preferences of outcomes and appropriate actions. Your values reflect on what's right and wrong. Your values to influence your behavior and attitudes. To know what your values are, look at the list below and check the box next to the values are important to you:

☐ Respect   ☐ Influence

☐ Poise   ☐ Acceptance

☐ Openness   ☐ Ambition

☐ Loyalty   ☐ Calmness

☐ Reputation   ☐ Cheerfulness

☐ Balance   ☐ Clarity

☐ Beauty   ☐ Credibility

☐ Boldness   ☐ Devotion

☐ Creativity   ☐ Elegance

☐ Fame   ☐ Empathy

☐ Humor   ☐ Flexibility

☐ Honesty   ☐ Honor

☐ Love   ☐ Independence

- [ ] Intimacy
- [ ] Keeness
- [ ] Leadership
- [ ] Knowledgeable
- [ ] Maturity
- [ ] Passion
- [ ] Persistence
- [ ] Playfulness
- [ ] Precision
- [ ] Prudence
- [ ] Restfulness
- [ ] Dedication
- [ ] Cooperation
- [ ] Forgiveness
- [ ] Tolerance
- [ ] Integrity
- [ ] Effort
- [ ] Self-control
- [ ] Sacrifice
- [ ] Simplicity
- [ ] Sophistication

- [ ] Tactfulness
- [ ] Gratitude
- [ ] Trustworthiness
- [ ] Variety
- [ ] Vigor
- [ ] Zeal
- [ ] Wisdom
- [ ] Wholesomeness
- [ ] Authenticity
- [ ] Zest
- [ ] Worthiness
- [ ] Victory
- [ ] Valor
- [ ] Traditionalism
- [ ] Thoroughness
- [ ] Temperance
- [ ] Success
- [ ] Strength
- [ ] Stability
- [ ] Spirituality
- [ ] Spontaneity

To live a fulfilling life, you must know what your values are. Do you cooperate with others? Is integrity important to you? Are you honest or do you lie a lot? Do you go to church? Do you say "thank you" when someone tries to do a nice thing for you?

Interest

Your interests include your hobbies and passions – activities that you like doing and things that you are curious about. To find out what your interests are, sit on a chair and take a deep breath. Then think about the things that concerns you. Are you concerned about the environment or fitness? Are you into farming? Do you like to spend your days in a gym? Do you like to write your thoughts and feelings? Do you like to create arts and crafts? What makes you forget about the time?

Temperament

Your temperament is your nature. It describes how you react and respond to the world. It is the foundation of your personality. Your temperament is not a passing mood or attitude. It remains constant throughout your life even when your personality changes.

There are four temperaments, namely:

1. Sanguine

Leona is a customer service representative at a designer store and she's good at her job. She takes care of her customers. She's friendly and accommodating. She's bold and brave. She once tried jumping off the plane (sky diving, of course) She also swam with the whale sharks when she was a teenager. Although Leona is intelligent, success is not that important to her. She just wants to have fun. Leona is a sanguine.

Sanguines are social butterflies. They like to be around people and they are generally easy to be around. They are optimistic, warm, people-oriented, and compassionate. They are flashy and bubbly. They have a good sense of humor and they are generally the life of the party.

Sanguines are pleasure-seekers. They crave for all good things in life. This could lead to credit card debts or becoming overweight. They are also unable to commit to anything as they prefer spontaneity over structure. They are more of a talker than a listener. They are expressive, dramatic, and they constantly love to be in the spotlight. They are naturally extroverted, so they flourish in the marketing, fashion, and entertainment industry. They also excel in team sports.

2. Melancholic

Melancholics are perfectionists. They are idealists and they have unrealistically high standards. They constantly criticize themselves and others. They are neurotic and they constantly overanalyze things and situations. They plan and think before they act. They also complain a lot and they are pessimistic. They always assume the worst.

They are naturally introverted and they prefer keeping an inner circle of a few trusted friends. They can be selfish, possessive, and intense. They are also very emotional – they are easily hurt and they can be moody. They are calm, but self-confident. They also pay attention to details.

Vincent Van Gough, Marie Curie, Albert Einstein, and Audrey Hepburn all have melancholic temperament. Accounting, management, and social work are perfect careers for people with melancholic temperament.

3. Choleric

Calista was born to a poor family in Queens. Her parents did not have enough money to send her to school, but she was persistent. When she was ten years old, she promised herself that she'll rise out of poverty. She worked on odd jobs to send herself to business school. Then, she built a manufacturing business from the ground up. She's driven and she would not let anyone stand in her way to success.

Calista became a millionaire before she turned 30. Although she's extremely attractive and wealthy, she's not likeable. She's bossy and she manipulates people to achieve her goals. She's extremely self-centered and she can be cruel. She has a low tolerance for bad performance. Calista has a choleric temperament.

Choleric people are irritable and short-tempered. They are goal-oriented, strong-willed, and decisive. They are well-organized and they are typically high achievers. They are persistent and they are great at handling emergency situations. They are also decisive and conceited.

People with choleric temperament are usually successful at whatever they do. But they can be arrogant and rude. They have the tendency to use other people to achieve their goals.

Vladimir Lenin, Alexander Hamilton, and Donald Trump all have choleric personality types.

4. Phlegmatic

Phlegmatic people are reserved, non-chalant, and relaxed. They are the walking definition of the word "chill". They have a good sense of humor and peaceful.

Phlegmatic leaders do not move as swiftly as choleric leaders, but they are more effective most of the time. They are great mediator. They are deliberate and it usually takes a while before they can make a decision. They are persistent and they are generally emotionally stable, empathetic, well-behaved, and trustworthy.

But, phlegmatic people tend to be indecisive and submissive. They find it hard to say no. They do not have the desire to win, they just want peace. They just want to lead a steady, calm, and quiet life. They do not stand out and they have the tendency to be self-righteous. They can be judgmental and passive-aggressive. They thrive industries like business management, programming, engineering, math, and technology.

Walt Disney, Bill Gates, Steve Wozniak, Abraham Lincoln, and Nikola Tesla are a few of the famous phlegmatic people.

Personal Strengths and Weakness

Your personal strengths consist of your talents, abilities, skills, and favorable personality traits. To get to know yourself better, you must be aware of your personal strengths. Are you intelligent, brave, or clever? Are you inspiring, logical, responsible, spontaneous, and persistent? What makes you lose track of time? What are the things that you can do effortlessly?

Doing an inventory of your personal strengths from time to time does not only increase your self-awareness. It also increases your self-confidence.

Nobody's perfect, so you must have a string of your personal weakness, too. Having a clear understanding of your weaknesses helps you grow. Are you reckless, messy, disorganized, or insensitive? Do you often procrastinate? Are you lazy and undisciplined?

Once, you have a clear understanding of your strengths and weaknesses, it's easier for you to focus on your areas of improvement. This understanding also allows you to keep doing what you're good at. If you're great at writing codes, it may be a good idea for you to become a computer programmer.

Life Mission

A life without purpose is an empty life. Everyone of us have a goal or a life mission. To live a happy life, you must be aware of what your life mission is and focus your energy in fulfilling that mission.

To identify your life mission, answer the following questions:

1. What do you want to achieve in five or ten years?

2. What areas of your life do you want to change?

3. What activities make you happy?

4. What makes you feel energized?

5. What activities make you lose track of time?

6. What makes you feel good about yourself?

7. What are you naturally good at?

8. What's your deepest desire?

9. What are your deepest values?

Sit on a chair and close your eyes. Then, visualize what your ideal life looks like. Just let your thoughts flow. Usually these visions reveal your desires, purpose, and mission.

Self-awareness is one of the best weapons that you can use against all the evils in the world. If you know who you are, it's easier for you to achieve your dreams and set boundaries. It's also easier for you to establish more meaningful relationships.

Tip #2: Reflect on Your Own Emotions

To increase your emotional intelligence, you must accurately identify your emotions. To do this, you need to go beyond the obvious to identify your feelings. Anger, for example, is an emotion that's characterized by antagonism. It is an intense emotion that increases your heart rate and elevates your blood pressure. We usually feel angry when someone crosses the line. But, we often mistake anger for other negative emotions such as frustration, impatience, annoyance, and irritation.

When you're feeling intense anger, ask yourself if you're really angry or you're simply grumpy, hungry, defensive, annoyed, irritated, or offended?

Like anger, sadness is also a general emotion. When you feel sad, you may be disillusioned, dismayed, paralyzed, disappointed, or regretful.

When you feel something, take time to think what that emotion really is. Are you hurt or jealous? Are you anxious or stressed? Are you happy or just simply thankful?

To improve your EQ, you must be able to precisely determine your feelings. You must also able to identify the intensity of your emotion and how you respond to certain situations.

How do you respond when:

- You get an angry email from your boss.

- When your spouse or lover blames you for something that's not your fault.

- When your co-worker cries unexpectedly.

- When you're tired after a long day at work.

- When another driver cuts you off on the road.

- When you move into a new home.

- When you get fired.

- When you don't have enough cash to pay your bills.

- When your kids get sick.

- When you are hungry.

- When you are reminded of a traumatic childhood memory.

- When you run into an ex-lover who hurt you deeply.

When you're aware of your emotions, you can easily manage them. So, take a few minutes every day to simply identify your emotions and analyze how you respond to them.

Tip #3: Pay Attention to Your Emotional Body Language

Your body is your temple. It is the most valuable possession you'll ever have. It is also your emotional compass. If you have a hard time identifying your emotions, you've got to listen to what your body is telling you. You have to pay attention to your emotional body language.

Here's a list of the common emotions and how your body reacts to them:

1. Anger

You normally clench your fist when you're angry. Your heart rate increases and you'll feel heat in your face and neck. You'd also clench your jaws and may feel headache and stomach ache.

2. Jealousy

That stomach pain that you've been experiencing lately may be caused by your inner green-eyed monster. Jealousy increases your blood pressure. It also causes pain in your gut by increasing the production of flight or fight hormones such as noradrenaline and adrenaline.

3. Sadness

Harry has gained weight in the last six months. He has been eating non-stop. He thought that he was just hungry. But, the truth is, Harry was depressed. He's struggling with emotional isolation and loneliness for a long time. He's in a rabbit hole and his only friend was food.

If you're sad, you'll feel a variety of negative symptoms. You'll feel headaches, back pains, muscle pain, exhaustion, and chest pains. You'll also experience weight gain.

4. Happiness

When you're happy, you feel giddy inside. It's like you're sliding on rainbows or floating in the air. Happiness is a positive emotion with positive physical symptoms. Studies show that happiness increases longevity. When you're happy, your muscles relax, and you have an open body language.

5. Fear

Fear is a powerful emotion that slowly kills your spirit and keeps you from living the life that you deserve.

When you're afraid, you do your best to stay in your comfort zone. This can keep you from growing and becoming the best that you could ever be. You say yes even when you mean no. You also procrastinate because you're afraid of rejection, judgment, uncertainty, criticism, and even success. You also get paralyzed and unable to make a decision.

When you're afraid, you'll experience different physical symptoms such as trembling, sweating, rapid heartbeat, dry mouth, nausea, clenched mouth, fidgeting, wide eyes, sweaty palms, dilated pupils, increase in blood pressure, and tensed muscles.

6. Shame

Shame is a strong negative emotion that can destroy your self-confidence and self-esteem. It is a dangerous emotion that can lead to inferiority complex. It also keeps you from living a free and happy life.

When you feel shame, your face is flushed and you are unable to maintain eye contact. You may also slouch.

7. Guilt

Are you often sleepless at night? Do you avoid the people you think you've wronged? Do you avoid eye contact? Are you often anxious and nervous? If you answered yes to most of these questions, you may be guilty of something.

Guilt increases your heart rate. It causes nausea and increases your body temperature. You may also have a bad posture.

Your body is your temple and your emotional compass. You should take care of it and you should listen to it.

Tip #4: Know When Enough is Enough

Vivian is a brilliant optometrist. She's kind and compassionate. But, she's also kind of a doormat. She has the intense need for approval. She's afraid to make mistakes and she does whatever she can to avoid conflict. She allows people to walk all over her. She feels that people only call her when they need her. She has no boundaries and so she ends up spreading herself too thin. Then, one day, she got fed up and had a nervous breakdown. She fell down the rabbit hole and unable to get out of it.

To thrive in life, you should know what you would and would not tolerate. You should draw the line.

People with high EQ know who they are. They know what they will and will not accept. To increase your emotional intelligence, you should know when enough is enough. You should be able to establish boundaries by following these steps:

1. You should develop a healthy respect for yourself.

Hey, you are important, too. Your needs are important, too. You should know that you're a valuable person. Take care of yourself and do not let other people define who you are. You should take responsibility and accountability for your life.

2. You should name your limits.

We all have limits. You can't set personal boundaries if you are not aware of what you can and cannot tolerate. Take time to identify your spiritual, physical, emotional, and mental limits.

How do you feel about lending money to your friends? Are you comfortable when someone touches you in a sexual way? Do you feel uncomfortable when someone shoves their spiritual beliefs down your throat?

3. Do not take responsibility for other people's emotions.

To live a happy and drama-free life, you should avoid taking responsibility for other people's emotions. You are not responsible for other people's drama and emotions. So, avoid giving unsolicited advice and do not feel guilty for other people's misfortunes.

4. Call out people who cross your personal boundaries.

If you feel that your co-worker or your spouse is not respecting your time, call him/her out. Communicate your boundaries with the people around you in a calm and dignified manner.

5. Stay away from people who do not respect your boundaries.

Some people would continuously cross your boundaries and if this happens, you've got to stay away. To increase your emotional intelligence and improve your mental health, you have to avoid people who don't respect your boundaries, time, and values.

Being aware of personal boundaries make it easier for you to manage your emotions. It also increases your self-esteem and self-respect.

Tip #5: Shift Your Focus Away From Yourself and Focus on Others

We all live inside an imaginary bubble. We all have our own world. We have the tendency to just focus on ourselves – our thoughts, needs, regrets, and sadness.

To increase your emotional intelligence, you should try to shift your focus away from yourself and focus on others.

1. Reduce your need for approval. You need to drop your "please validate and notice me" mentality.

2. Take time to observe the people around you – their posture, facial expressions, and tone of voice. This will help you identify what they're feeling.

3. In this modern world, we are all taught not to give a damn about other people. But, it is important to give a damn. To increase your emotional intelligence, it's important to try to understand other people.

4. Be there for others when you're needed. Take time to listen to the people you care about.

5. Pay attention to overall appearance. Take time to notice other people's appearance. Are they wearing casual clothes? Or are they wearing power suits? People who dress for success are usually ambitious while people who wear casual clothes are more spirited and laid back.

6. Check the posture. People who hold their head high are confident and are happier with their lives. But, in some cases, these people may also have a big ego. People who slouch usually lack self-esteem or may be depressed.

7. Observe their movements for they say a lot about their emotions, beliefs, and perceptions. If a person leans towards you, it means he likes you. If a person is hiding his hands, it means that he is lying or hiding something. If you see someone biting his lips or nails, he might be anxious, worried, or under pressure.

    To get to know other people better and connect to them, you have to habitually observe their movements and facial expressions. A happy person tends to smile or laugh while a sad person's mouth may be slightly turned down, like a pout.

    Here's a list of common microexpressions and movements associated with emotions:

- Anger – aggressive body language, walking with exaggerated swinging of arms, disapproving frowns, clenching fist, sudden movements, snarling, flushed face.

- Anxiety – cold sweat, fidgeting, voice tremors, shaking, no eye contact, high pulse, crossed arms, damp eyes, trembling lips, and pale face.

- Shame – flushed face or false smile.

- Happiness – smiling, bright eyes, relaxation of muscles, and open body language.

- Surprise – open mouth, wide eyes, backward movement, and raised eyebrows.

People around you are fighting battles that you know nothing about. To empathize with other people and fully understand them, you have to be curious about other people's feelings.

Being curious about other people's feelings can help you build deeper connections and it allows you to empathize with them.

In your office, observe your co-workers – how they dress, their posture, the tone of their voice, and their disposition. Are they smiling? Do they have aggressive body language? How do they speak? Pay attention to verbal and non-verbal cues.

Tip #6: Stop Peddling Your Soul for A Pay Check

Stress is a silent killer. It can keep you from living the life that you want and deserve. It can destroy your health, too. Too much stress can take a toll on your emotional health and could significantly decrease your emotional intelligence.

So, to increase your emotional intelligence, you've got to stop selling your soul for a pay check.

If your work is slowly killing you inside, you just have to take a step back. Do you often feel lost? Do you think that you've stopped growing? Are you not happy with your work? If so, then it might be time to quit and get a job that feeds your spirit.

Remember that it's silly to lose your sanity over a job. If you feel that your work is sucking your soul and making you angrier by the minute, you should consider getting a new one. Find a job that excites you and gives you a strong sense of purpose. What do you really want to do? What makes you lose track of time? What do you want to be known for?

Tip #7: Identify Your Emotional Triggers

Emotional triggers are events, people, words, things, and situations that evoke certain emotions.

To effectively manage your emotions, you have to identify what triggers them. Knowing your emotional triggers allow you to balance your emotions and logic. Remember, you can't control other people, their thoughts, actions, and behaviors, but you can control how you react to them.

Not knowing your emotional triggers will make it hard for you to regulate your emotions. It helps you deal with painful emotions in a healthy and dignified manner.

Sit in a chair and take a deep breath. Close your eyes and imagine that you are in the workplace. Someone is asking you to do something that you do not want to do. How do you feel? Do you feel deep resentment? Do you feel anger? Do you feel like you are violated in some ways? Take time to identify and feel your emotions. If you feel an intense and pounding emotion in your chest, then being asked to do something you don't want to do can trigger anxiety and anger.

Take another deep breath. Now, imagine that someone is giving you a gift. Visualize yourself unwrapping the gift. Do you feel loved or appreciated? Do you feel intense gratitude? Do you feel shame, like you don't deserve the gift? Take a minute or two to examine your emotions. Feel those emotions.

Now, think about your pet dog, if you have one. Do you feel happy when you think about your dog? Do you feel guilty? Do you feel worried that you're not taking good care of your pet?

Shift your mind back to your workplace. How do you feel when your co-worker is disrespecting you. Do you feel intense anger? Do you feel like you're going to explode? Do you allow these disrespectful comments to get to you? Do you feel shame? Do you feel small?

Now, let's explore deeper emotional triggers. Imagine that your closest friend landed her dream job. She's now earning six figures a month. Do you feel jealous? Do you feel resentment? Do you feel like you deserve success more than her? Do you feel anxious that you're not where you're supposed to be in life?

Take time to listen to what you feel after you read each phrase. This will help you determine your deepest emotional triggers.

You can also identify your emotional triggers by answering the following questions:

1. *What makes you feel loved?*

2. *What makes you angry?*

3. *What makes you happy? What makes your heart leap with joy?*

4. *What annoys you?*

5. *What makes you afraid?*

6. *What makes you feel guilty? Do you have hidden feelings of guilt?*

7. *What makes you sad?*

8. *What drives you crazy?*

Identifying your emotional triggers gives you a strong sense of control. It allows you to respond appropriately to uncomfortable situations. It also helps you achieve emotional growth and maturity.

Do Not React To Your Emotional Triggers Right Away

To avoid becoming a slave to your emotions, you have to react in a healthy way. If you react to an emotional trigger right away, you may say something that you regret. Take Greg as an example. Greg is an emotionally available bachelor who never met his mother. So all his life, he's craving for a mother's love but he is unaware of this. He is also a successful businessman who has no plans of settling down anytime. He is at a time of his life where he wants to just date women and have fun. Then, he met a woman named Lola.

Lola is a lovely girl and she has a strong maternal instinct. She is kind but she had been heart broken far too many times. After sleeping together for the first time, Lola prepared a hot meal for Greg. He was surprised because no one ever did that before, he was used to eating microwaveable meals. He felt an intense feeling of joy that he cannot control, so he blurted the words "I love you". But, he did not mean those words. He was just caught up in the moment. That awkward moment was the turning point of their relationship. Greg began to pull away and Lola was heartbroken once more.

The best way to control your emotion is to delay your reaction. Delaying your reaction allows you to respond to emotional triggers in a calm and logical manner.

When you hear something that makes you angry, take a deep breath. Do not react right away. Count from one to ten and keep breathing. Think before you open your mouth so you would not say something that you would regret later on.

Tip #8: Learn to Manage Stress

As mentioned earlier in this book, stress decreases your ability to control your emotions. When you're stressed, you're more likely to feel anxious and depressed. You'll have mood swings.

Stress does not only decrease your emotional intelligence, it can also cause serious health problems such as neck pain, tension headaches, anxiety, gastrointestinal problems, obesity, insomnia, chronic fatigue, arthritis, diabetes, and high blood pressure.

To increase your emotional intelligence, you must learn to manage stress. Here's a list of 100 action items that you can do to reduce stress.

- Watch an inspirational movie. You can watch "Life is Beautiful (La Vita e Bella)" or a famous Indian movie called "Three Idiots". These movies give you hope and help you get through a bad day.

- Doodle on a paper using a paint or crayons.

- Get enough sleep. You'll have a problem controlling your emotions if you lack sleep.

- Say "no" more often to avoid spreading yourself too thin.

- Use your time wisely. Stay away from things that waste your time.

- Unclutter your life. Organize your bedroom and your workspace.

- Watch funny videos on YouTube.

- Read an inspirational book.

- Write down quotes from an inspirational book.

- Look at the stars.

- Sing a happy song.

- Whistle. Whistling reduces stress and it makes you happier.

- Make your own travel journal.

- Go to a place you've never been.

- Get to work early.

- Get up early so you have enough time.

- Listen to relaxing music and happy tunes.

- Kiss or hug someone you love.

- Go outside and feel the sun on your face.

- Dance like no one is watching.

- Try aromatherapy. Lavender scent helps reduce stress.

- Get a massage.

- Drink hot tea.

- Do yoga.

- Eat a small piece of dark chocolate.

- Do a digital detox and turn off your smart phone.

- Whenever you feel overwhelmed, take a nap.

- Go swimming as it is extremely relaxing.

- Look at some cat photos.

- Go for a walk.

- Do not trade your sleep for work. Your health is more important than your work.

- Do not create unnecessary drama in your life.

- Do not try to do everything by yourself. Try to get some help whenever needed and learn how to delegate.

- Stop worrying.

- Take a long bath.

- Do something that you're passionate about.

- Simplify your life.

- Always take your bathroom and lunch break.

- Stop smoking.

- Be patient.

- Learn to prioritize.

- Talk to a trusted friend.

- Play with your pet.

- Go to a museum.

- Drink more water.

- Exchange jokes with a friend.

- Grab a quick snack.

- Squeeze a stress ball.

- Drink a glass of orange juice daily.

- Go to a sauna.

- If you have a close relationship with your mom, call her. This helps release stress.

- Close your email. Do not check it for a few days.

- Drink black tea. It is extremely relaxing.

- If you have a toxic job, start looking for a new one.

- Walk to work.

- Eat a bowl of colorful and delicious fruits.

- Float in water.

- Take a trip to the nearest beach.

- Go to a quiet place.

- Just let it all out.

- Do not drink coffee. It makes you feel more agitated.

- Keep a journal and write about your daily experiences.

- Tickle your pet dog or cat.

- Stop a bad habit.

- Make copies of important documents. This will save you a lot of time.

- Buy new clothes. But, do this only once in a while. Shopping therapy is not a good solution to stress.

- Learn a new language or acquire a new skill.

- Buy some art.

- Get a haircut.

- Get some fresh air.

- Walk around the park.

- If you can afford it, go to Iceland. It is one of the most beautiful countries in the world.

- Set priorities. This will save you from stressful situations later on.

- Ask for help.

- Walk in the rain. It feels good.

- Hug a friend for no reason.

- Hum a popular jingle.

- Go on a picnic with a loved one.

- Watch a good movie and eat home-cooked popcorn.

- Praise other people.

- Remember that you always have a choice. You can always get out of a situation that you don't like.

- Stop trying to fix other people.

- Spray vanilla essential oil in your bedroom before you go to sleep.

- Connect with nature as often as you can.

- Move on from anything that no longer serve you.

- Get out of debt.

- Say less and listen more.

- Travel more.

- Laugh every day.

- Pay your credit card every month. This can save you a lot of stress.

- Spray fruity scents.

- Take a salsa class.

- Repaint your room.

- Grow a plant.

- Try surfing.

- Eat a lot of vegetables and fruits.

- Go skiing during the winter season.

- Try skating.

- Aim low. If you set your standards too high, you'll get disappointed too often.

It's easier for you to master and control your emotions when you're relaxed. After a long day at work, kick off your shoes and watch a good movie. It's good for your emotional health.

Tip #9: Learn How to Handle Difficult People

To save your sanity, stay away from toxic people or energy vampires. But, how do you spot these people? These are the most common characteristics of toxic people:

- They tend to be judgmental. They will criticize other people to make them feel bad about themselves.

- They don't apologize when they are wrong.

- They are manipulative.

- They make you work for their approval.

- They are always right.

- They complain constantly.

- They take up too much of your time.

- They create drama.

- They will lie to you constantly.

- They are self-absorbed.

- They play the victim.

- They can be temperamental.

- They lack compassion.

- They treat you poorly.

- They put you down.

- They blame you for their problems.

- They are defensive.

- They do not keep their promises.

- They have anger issues.

- They exploit you.

- They are bitter and vindictive.

- They rush you into doing things.

- They withhold affection.

- They are selfish and stingy.

- Use flattery or money to control you.

- They play games.

To protect your self-esteem, you have to stay away from toxic people and surround yourself with people who love you for who you are. Surround yourself with people who inspire you to become a better person.

It's hard to manipulate you if you have a positive self-image. Having self-confidence increases your power to regulate your emotions.

Tip #10: Bounce Back from Adversity

Resilience is a sign of high emotional intelligence. It is defined as the ability to bounce back from adversity.

Resilience helps you hold on to your dreams, even when faced with difficulties. It helps you move forward from a traumatic event and it keeps you in the driver seat of your life. It helps you take advantage of post-traumatic growth.

Resilience is an invisible muscle that you can develop over time by following these steps:

1. Derive meaning from a difficult situation.

This may sound like a cliché, but everything happens for a reason. If you let your emotions get the best of you, you'll never be able to rise up from a traumatic event. You just have to stop and give meaning to what's happening to you.

J.K. Rowling was jobless, depressed, and separated from her husband when she was in her early thirties. She was poor and her mental health was deteriorating. But, she had a big idea and a lot of talent. And so, she wrote the first Harry Potter book. Today, Harry Potter is considered as a literary gem that people of all ages love. If J.K. Rowling succeeded in her office job, she would not have the time to write Harry Potter.

Let's take a look at the story of Elizabeth, a PR executive. Three years ago, Elizabeth's sister died of breast cancer. It really broke her heart, but she chose to make the best out of the situation. She built a foundation for breast cancer patients who can't afford treatment. She met a great man named Harry in one of her fundraising events. They got married a year later.

Remember that there's always a reason why things happen. There's always a reason why we lose the people we love.

2. See your hardship as an opportunity.

Here's the truth, a challenge is an opportunity. It is an opportunity for you to grow and become stronger. It's an opportunity for you to make better decisions, learn from your mistakes, and become wiser.

3. Focus on what you can control.

You can't control everything that happens in your life. This is why it is important to focus on what you can control.

4. Imagine a positive outcome.

Visualization is a powerful tool that you can use to attract your desired outcome. It also gives you hope and it helps you relax during challenging times. So, when you're on the verge of an emotional breakdown, close your eyes and imagine a positive outcome. Imagine yourself rising above your current situation and achieving everything that you could ever hope for in life.

Life kicks our ass every once in a while. So, you've got to develop that invisible muscle called resilience so you would have the strength to fight back.

Tip #11: Control Your Temper

Mel Gibson is a charismatic actor. But, he has serious anger issues. He is a known racist and homophobic. When he got arrested for driving under the influence, he blurted out anti-Semitic remarks. He also has a long history of domestic abuse, calling his ex-wife a gold-digger and a whore.

Mel Gibson is good-looking and talented, but that's not enough to make it in the entertainment industry. You must have good people skills, too. The public had enough of Gibson's rants and temper. So, now, he virtually has no career.

If you want to succeed in life, you have to learn how to control your temper. You can do so by following these tips:

1. Think before you speak. This will keep you from saying things that you will regret later on. It's best to count one to ten before you respond to something that makes you angry.

2. If you think you're going to explode any minute, take a step back and go somewhere quiet. You can also put on a pair of earplugs and listen to good music.

3. Repeat relaxing words such as "take it easy".

4. When you're ready, express your anger in a healthy way. You can scream on a pillow or go for a run to release the negative energy. You can also vent out to a trusted friend. You can also release tension by doing creative activities like painting or dancing.

5. Stop talking about things that make you angry and stay away from things that trigger your anger. Learn to let go of your angry thoughts as they do not serve you.

If your temper is getting out of hand, it may be a good idea to get professional help.

Tip #12: Manage Your Impulses

Impulse control is a powerful emotional intelligence competency that you can use to solve problems and build a successful life. It reflects your ability to show restraint when faced with temptations. It also reflects your ability to control aggression and display irresponsible behavior.

Impulse management increases your credibility and trustworthiness. It also increases your conscientiousness, adaptability, and self-understanding. If you can't control your impulses, you may suffer from the following symptoms:

- Obesity

- Aggression

- Stealing

- Lying

- Depression

- Obsessive thoughts

- Lack of patience

- Anxiety

- Criminal behavior

If you don't have the ability to control your impulses, you have the tendency to jump to conclusions and send emotionally charged text messages or emails.

To control your impulses, you need to:

1. Practice self-discipline. Do not wait until you're in the mood to do things.

2. Eat healthy.

3. You must make a conscious decision to take small actions to bring you closer to your goals. Do you want to run? Run for 10 minutes. Do you have a report due? Write a few paragraphs. The key to self-discipline is to just get started.

4. If you struggle with ADHD, do interval training. Focus on your work for five minutes and then, give yourself five minutes to do something else. Then, increase your work time to ten minutes. Take another five minute break. After the break, focus on your work for 30 minutes. This strategy helps you get started and finish the task at hand.

5. Celebrate your success. Give yourself a cookie after writing a 10,000 word report. You deserve it!

Managing your impulses is not as hard as you think. So, control your impulses now before they control you.

Tip #13: Practice Humility

No one wants likes conceited people. To increase your emotional intelligence and likeability, you must practice humility.

According to studies, humble people exhibit higher self control. They have better work performance, higher grades, and better relationships. They are also less judgmental.

But, what is humility? True humility is not about thinking less of yourself. It is about thinking about yourself less. It is the exact opposite of narcissism and pride. Humble people do not have a problem admitting their mistakes.

If you're a naturally proud person, here's a list of tips that you can use to cultivate humility:

1. Have a clear assessment of your self-worth. Humble people are self-confident, too. They know their worth, so they do not see the need of putting other people down just to validate their importance.

2. Put other people first.

3. Do not speak about yourself too much.

4. Learn to accept feedback.

5. Do not seek admiration.

6. Help other people succeed.

7. Learn from other people.

Humility allows you to easily connect with others. It also increases the level of your happiness.

Tip #14: Find Out Why People Act The Way They Do

Christopher and Celine have been married for two years. They have a great house and they love each other so much. But, they have one problem. Christopher is a jealous man. He gets mad when Celine talks to other men.

Celine cannot understand why Chris is jealous all the time. One day, she had enough of Chris' jealousy so she left him.

But, here's the truth about Chris. When he was in high school, he fell in love with a woman named Taylor. They were together for three years until he caught her in bed with his best friend. It crushed him. He wanted to trust Celine, but the pain caused by Taylor's betrayal was too deep. If Celine took the time to get Chris to open up about Taylor, she could have saved her marriage.

Here's the harsh truth- the world does not revolve around you. You have to stop taking things personally and find out why people act the way that they do. This helps you understand other people at a deeper level. For example, your boss does not micromanage you because you're incompetent. She micromanages her staff because she's afraid of not being in control. Your daughter does not lie because she thinks that you are unworthy of her respect. She lies because she feels inadequate and she's afraid of disappointing you.

Observe other people's behavior and then, take time to identify the root cause behind their behaviors. This does not only increase your emotional intelligence, it also allows you to build deeper and more meaningful relationships.

Tip #15: Learn to Take Constructive Criticisms

Do you go on defensive mode when someone is giving you feedback? Do you have a hard time accepting your weaknesses? If so, you have low emotional intelligence.

Some people would criticize you to put you down and make you feel bad about yourself. But some people would criticize you to help you improve. You should shut out destructive criticisms. But, you must also learn to take constructive criticisms.

When, someone's giving you a feedback, you need to follow these tips:

1. Take a deep breath and listen to every word the other person is saying. Do not dismiss the feedback and try to listen for understanding.

2. Express gratitude and say thank you to the other person for giving you feedback. You can simply say, "I really appreciate that you're taking the time to discuss this matter with me. Thank you for your feedback". This does not mean that you agree with the other person's assessment. It just means that you are mature enough to handle feedback.

3. Do not take the criticism personally. A negative feedback is not an insult. It is just an observation.

4. Ask the person giving you feedback to help on how to improve your weak areas.

5. Create an action plan and present your progress. This way, the other person knows that you are truly working on your areas of improvement.

Remember that constructive criticism is good for you. So, you have to leave your ego at the door and take time to listen to feedback. This allows you to maximize your growth potential.

Tip #16: Practice Empathy

Empathy is a skill that allows you to connect with other people in a much deeper level. It motivates altruism and it allows you to truly care about other people. It builds trust and it helps you develop meaningful friendships.

Here's a list of tips that you can use to develop empathy:

1. Listen.

Listening does not only allow you to establish a profound connection with another person. It also increases your knowledge and it allows you to understand other people's perspective. Listening intensifies the conversation and it also saves money. If your job involves negotiating with other people or a group of people, listening is an important skill to learn because it allows you to overcome resistance. It also helps you make sound decisions.

When you talk to someone, look into his eyes and try to listen to every word he says. Nod while he his talking so he knows that you are really listening to him. If he's relaying an instruction, make sure to recap to ensure that you understood the instruction clearly. This habit increases your efficiency, especially if you're in a client partnership or customer service industry. This reduces misunderstanding and improves your relationships. It also helps you uncover opportunities.

If you're in a relationship with someone, never discourage your partner when he/she is airing his/her concerns. Listening may help you save your relationship.

2. Be tolerant.

People are raised in different environments. Everyone goes through different unique experiences every day. To increase your emotional intelligence, you have to be more tolerant of other people's views.

If someone is voicing out an opinion that's different from yours, learn to hear them out, without prejudice. Try to understand the other person's point of view and then, agree to disagree.

For instance, you despise President Donald Trump, but your friend is a die-hard Trump supporter. Before you engage in a heated argument with your friend try to listen to his views. He has his reasons for supporting the man, and you have your own reasons for not. After hearing him out, agree to disagree. You can say something like *"I understand where you are coming from, but I strongly disagree with that point of view. But, I understand you and it's okay to disagree from time to time. We can have different views and still remain friends."*

3. Show vulnerability.

To put yourself into other people's shoes, you also need to show your own vulnerability. You have to keep it real and openly communicate your needs.

If someone is sharing a difficult experience with you, listen intently and let him know that you understand. Then, show your vulnerability and share your own experiences. For example, if a coworker shares her difficult relationship with her parents, listen carefully and express your understanding. Then, share your own experience and how challenging your relationship with your mother is. This does not only increases your empathy, it also allows you to deepen your relationship with the other person.

4. Try to understand other people's perspectives.

People have different upbringings and everyone grew up in different environments. So, it's normal that we have different perspectives. To increase your empathy and emotional intelligence, you have to try to understand other people's perspectives, even if they are different from yours. Once you see why other people believe what they believe in, validate it. Remember that validation is not the same as agreement. You can accept other people's beliefs without agreeing with them.

5. Encourage other people.

Do not walk on other people's dreams. Encourage the people you love to follow their dreams and pursue the things that they are passionate about.

For instance, your thirty year-old friend tells you that she wants to start a career as a singer. Instead of telling her that it's impossible for a newcomer her age to make it big in the music industry, simply encourage her. Give her the strength to take small steps towards her dreams. You can help her find a part time lounge singer job in hotels and casinos. You can also encourage her to take voice lessons to hone her talent.

6. Smile at other people.

A smile has a magical effect on people. It releases happy hormones and it makes you more likeable. It also makes you seem approachable.

7. Try another person's life for a minute.

For example, you're a successful accountant. You have a stable job and you like routines. You have a number of friends who are digital nomads. To understand your friends, try living their life once in a while. Work on freelance projects while you're travelling or on a vacation. This will help you understand them more.

8. Try mirroring other people.

Mirroring other people help you enter their spirits. It helps you persuade or influence them.

People are natural narcissists. For example, you probably like seeing yourself in other people. You are more likely to listen to people who look like you, talk like you, or share your point of view.

If you aspire to be a leader, you must have the ability to influence others. And you can do this by mirroring other people.

First, you have to maintain eye contact. This makes the other person feel like they have your complete attention. It makes them feel like they are the center of the universe at the moment.

Now, triple nod when you listen. Then, start mimicking the other person's actions. If the other person scratches his head, scratch yours. You can also mimic the other person's tone of voice and speech style.

Mirroring builds trust. You can use it to develop empathy and emotional intelligence. You can also use it to influence others. You can use this technique in various situations. You can use this when talking to your boss or when you're trying to convince your subordinates to see your point of view. You can also use this in handling a difficult situation.

When you're trying to influence other people, mirror their words, vocal tone, pace, body language, hand gesture, and even the way they dress. If your partner uses the word "awesome" too many times, try to use that word often, too.

9. Treat other people the way they want to be treated.

Remember the Golden Rule, *"treat other people the way you want to be treated"*. If you want to cultivate richer and deeper relationships, you have to treat other people the way you want to be treated.

Observe the people around you and pay attention to what they want deep in their hearts. Do they want respect? Do they want assurance or validation? Do they want to experience independence? Do they have the strong desire for inclusion? Do they want to increase their social status? Do they want peace?

If a subordinate asks for a little independence and self-reliance, stop micromanaging him. Do not breathe down on his neck. Give him enough freedom to exercise his creativity. Give him space.

10. Use empathy statements.

When you're talking to someone who is experiencing intense emotions, it's best to use empathy statements. These statements make the other person feel valued and understood.

Here's a list of phrases that you can use to express your empathy. But, only use these statements if you mean them:

- *"If I were you, I would feel the same way, too."*

- *"I understand you."*

- *"I get you. You are totally making sense."*

- *"You are right."*

- *"That sounds frustrating. If I were in your position right now, I'd feel frustrated, too."*

- *"You must be really hurt."*

- *"That sounds scary."*

- *"I agree with you."*

- *"You're doing great."*

- *"That's difficult, but I like how you handled it."*

- *"That must be really frightening."*

- *"That was not easy."*

- *"I hear you."*

- *"I feel you."*

- *"I am sorry that this happened."*

- *"That is so disappointing."*

- *"No wonder you feel that way."*

- *"Whatever you decide, I support you."*

- *"I know how that feels."*

- *"I know how frustrating that must be."*

- *"That's sad."*

- *"I've been through the same thing, so I understand you."*

- *"I would have done the same thing."*

- *"Yes, that's a difficult situation to be in."*

- *"I understand why you are angry."*

- *"If I were you, I'd be angry, too."*

- *"That's devastating!"*

- *"You have valid points."*

- *"I see why you feel that way."*

- *"That's totally frustrating."*

Empathy helps you build deeper relationships. It increases your influence on others. It also allows you to make new friends.

Tip #17: Use Humor to Relieve Your Tension

Use humor to relieve tension and gain control over your emotions. Humor relieves pain and it makes you more likeable, too.

Humor also makes you persuasive. It reduces hostility and it helps you deflect criticisms. It also distracts you from negative emotions. Most of all, it makes you feel good.

Try to find something funny in a difficult situation. Use humor to deflect tension. Let's say, you lost your luggage at the airport. To diffuse your anger and frustration, try to think about how silly you look when you found out that you lost your bags. If this does not work, try to think about something funny like a video you've seen on YouTube.

Also, try a new craze called laughter yoga. This yoga type increases your happiness and it also helps you cope with unpleasant circumstances. Laughter yoga relaxes your body and it helps you deal with painful emotions in a healthy way. It makes you more grounded and it helps you gain clarity.

To do this, sit on a chair. Then, start clapping or making faces. Be silly. Be childlike. Now, think about something funny. Then, start laughing from your stomach. Just laugh out loud. Laugh like you're crazy.

Then, chant the word "yay". After a few minutes, you'll feel more relaxed. You'll feel that joy surging from deep within you.

This exercise may seem silly, but it's a good emotion management technique. It helps relieve tension and pain. It makes you happier, too.

Tip #18: Go Oooommm

When you're stressed out, you'll lose a sense of who you are. When this happens, your emotional intelligence decreases.

Meditation helps you stay in tune with your spirit by decreasing stress. This practice increases your happiness and it increases self-acceptance. It also helps you manage your emotions by downplaying negative feelings such as loneliness, anger, depression, and fear. It helps you stay calm in stressful situations.

To practice meditation:

1. Find a private area where you can practice meditation. It's good to meditate near the beach or in the middle of the forest. But, you can practice meditation in the comfort of your home. You can build a meditation area inside your bedroom and decorate it with scented candles and cushions.

2. Wear comfortable clothing and turn off your gadgets.

3. Sit on a cushion or on a chair. Close your eyes and take deep breaths.

4. Then, listen to your breathing. Notice how your chest rises and falls as you inhale and exhale. Focus on your breathing. If your mind starts to wander, redirect your mind back to your breath.

5. Now, observe your thoughts. When you're alone, what do you think about? Do you worry about the future? Do you think about food? Do you think about what to wear?

6. Observe your emotions. Ask yourself, "how do I feel"? Are you sad or depressed? Is there a hole in your being that you cannot explain? Do you feel happy or blissful? Are you content with your life? Are you unhappy with how your life turned out?

7. Take time to feel these emotions. Don't just silence them. Feel them, acknowledge them, and then release them. Remember that all emotions are beautiful, even anger or sadness. So, take time to process these emotions. Take as much time as you need.

8. Keep taking deep breaths as you watch your thoughts closely. Do this for about five minutes.

9. Open your eyes.

Practicing meditation daily decreases your flight or fight response to stress. It increases your ability to control yourself and your emotions during challenging times. It also increases your optimism and it helps you resist destructive urges.

Meditation does not only increases your emotional intelligence, it also helps you achieve that one thing everyone wants – peace of mind. To reap the optimum benefits of meditation, practice meditation daily. You don't have to set aside a lot of time for meditation. You can simply meditate for five minutes daily.

Tip #19: Practice Social Responsibility

Practicing social responsibility does not only improve your personal karma. It also allows you to enjoy high levels of emotional experience. You can practice social responsibility in many ways, including:

1. Respect the rights of others. Do not step on other people's toes.

2. Be honest and trustworthy.

3. Volunteer in community projects. You can join a fund-raising project, plant trees, or simply pick up the trash in your neighborhood.

4. Be compassionate. Take time to listen to the people around you and try to reach out to them. Smile more and practice good manners. Remember that simple things can mean so much to the people around you.

5. Be a good neighbor. If you want to be seen as a mature and emotionally intelligent person, you must be good to your neighbors by considering their lifestyle. If your neighbors work in the night shift, do not play loud music during day time.

6. Respect other people's property and return things that you borrowed.

Little things can mean so much at the people around you. So, make sure that you practice social responsibility day in and day out.

Tip #20: Develop Grit

Grit is the ability to stay focused on a goal. It is a combination of courage, self-discipline, conscientiousness, endurance, resilience, self-confidence, optimism, creativity, passion, and perseverance. It is the ability to keep going even when faced with difficult circumstances. Grit is also known as mental strength.

According to psychologists, grit is the key to success. It is a quality that's more important than IQ.

To develop your grit, you can use these tips:

1. Pursue things that you're truly passionate about.

It's easy to stick to something that you're passionate about. To increase your mental strength, focus on things that you are passionate about. Get a job that excites you.

2. Choose hope and optimism.

Even when things are not going well, choose to stay hopeful. Believe that better days are coming. Always choose to look at the brighter side of things.

3. Surround yourself with gritty people.

To become more motivated, you have to surround yourself with people who have the ability to persevere.

4. Practice conscientiousness.

Do your best all the time. Be organized and practice self-discipline. Do the things that you say you would do. Do not give up when things get hard.

5. Keep going.

A number of publishers thought that Harry Potter was not good enough. What would have happened if J.K. Rowling gave up? Bookworms would not have the opportunity to read one of the most precious modern literary gems.

You'll get rejected from time to time. You'll also experience failure at some point. But, if you want to achieve great success in life, you have to keep going. You must never give up.

6. Embrace change.

Change is sometimes uncomfortable. But, it is necessary. If you want to grow as a person, you have to learn to embrace change.

Change is sometimes unpleasant, but it is good for you. It allows you to step out of your comfort zone and expand your horizon.

7. Focus on the solution.

Instead of focusing on the problem, focus on the solution. Dig deeper and address the underlying causes of your problems.

8. Be brave.

To increase your self-motivation and grit, you have to be brave. You have to make bold decisions. Remember- no guts, no glory. You cannot achieve great success unless you're brave.

Self-motivation allows you to endure difficult circumstance. It empowers you to keep going even if you're faced with disappointments and failure.

People with low EQ easily give up on their dreams. But, people with high EQ choose to get going and wear their failures as battle scars.

Tip #21: Do Things Differently

One of the most effective techniques that you can use to increase your emotional intelligence is to try new experiences and step out of your comfort zone.

Stepping out of your comfort zone pushes you to use your untapped knowledge and resourcefulness. It helps you get to know yourself a little more intimately. It also helps you to grow.

Make a change in your daily routine. You can simply use another shampoo or take a different route to work. If you're comfortable with taking bigger risks, do it. You can travel to new places you have not been before. Travelling helps you discover things about yourself. It uncovers your inner joy.

Taking risks enhances your emotional intelligence by increasing your self-awareness. It also reduces the anxiety associated with risks. It helps you grow and increases your maturity.

Conclusion

Thank you again for the purchase of this book.

I hope that this book was able to increase your emotional intelligence. Now, let's do a quick review of what you've learned in this book:

- ✓ Emotional intelligence is an important trait. It is the key to success. Many psychologists think that EQ is even more important than IQ.

- ✓ To increase your emotional intelligence, you have to be aware of your emotions.

- ✓ Take time to feel your emotions. Remember that all emotions are beautiful.

- ✓ Make a list of your strengths and weaknesses.

- ✓ Set goals. Setting goals do not only increase your motivation. It also increases your ability to regulate your emotions.

- ✓ Do not react to your emotions right away. If you're feeling an intense negative emotion, count from one to ten before you react.

- ✓ Replace your negative emotions with positive ones.

- ✓ Empathize with the people around you. Empathy allows you to build more meaningful relationships. It also increases your influence and likability.

- ✓ Develop grit.

Emotional intelligence is something that you can develop over time. It helps you manage difficult situations. It helps you express yourself clearly and it helps you gain respect from others.

Book – III

Cognitive Behavioral Therapy

The Definitive Guide to Understanding Your Brain,

Depression, Anxiety and How to Overcome It

Introduction

I want to thank you and congratulate you for downloading Cognitive Behavioral Therapy: The Definitive Guide to Understanding Your Brain, Depression, Anxiety and How to Overcome It.

Depression and anxiety are two very difficult behavioral conditions for patients suffering from their negative effects. They are both difficult to identify and to treat. There are a range of medications and behavioral therapy treatments available, but each method comes with their own challenges, and what might work for one person could prove to be utterly ineffective for another. Compounding the complexity of this issue is the inherent scale on which these problems exist; what could prove to be debilitating for one person is just an inconvenience for another. To share an experience of what depression or anxiety truly feels like is impossible, and often the treatment takes so long to be effective that the sliding scale of improvement makes true analysis of one's progress troublesome.

I decided to write this book to give readers insight into the larger issues surrounding depression and anxiety. I have been suffering with these conditions all my life, and have tried nearly every technique available to try and improve my mental health. Today I live a healthy life, a steady life, but this was not easily obtained. Through all of my treatments, seeing different doctors in separate branches of the medical community, I've come to the realization that there is a first step in combating anxiety and depression, understating. A patient must realize the base root of their anxiety and depression for them to ever get a true handle on how to treat it. This will not make every problem of theirs go away, but it will make the overall process of treatment much easier.

Understanding the mechanics of the human brain in how they relate to anxiety and depression is paramount to being able to improve one's life. This does not need to be a complicated affair, but rather human history needs to be put into perspective of how humans evolved and how mental health conditions came more prominent with advances in technology and ever-progressive social constructs.

Once you have an understanding for how the human brain has come to terms with anxiety and depression in the modern era, you can more effectively treat these mental health concerns. The advice I offer is practical, and comes down to regimenting our bodies in a way similar to our ancestry. It is my hope that by the completion of this book you have a better understanding of what causes anxiety and depression, as well as have a toolbox for how to overcome and treat these illnesses.

If anxiety and depression have proven to be a point of difficulty in your life, then look no further. Keep reading and in a few chapters you will have a better understanding of complex background that affects these conditions; you will have strategies for how to minimize the impact of these mental health concerns, and you will feel confident that you can take your life back into your own hands.

Ryan James

Chapter 1: From Forests to the Urban Sprawl

A Generalized Theory of Anxiety

As our lives become more comfortable, as our standard of living increases, our lives are becoming ever more static. We have routines that take us from our waking hours until we sleep at night. Each day we go through actions that are similar to the day before. There are breaks in this routine, but they are seldom major changes. It may not be the only factor, but a major cause of modern day anxiety is related to the routine of our lives and the static environments in which we spend most of our time.

The first time I heard of theory of static environments being an agitator of anxiety in humans I was skeptical, but over time I have come to appreciate the complexity of this well thought out argument. The basic premise behind the cause of anxiety in modern day humans is that our brains have evolved to be sensitive to minor changes in our environment. This refers to temperature changes over the course of a few days, or a small change like the rattling of a bush in our vision when we are in the woods. The brain has developed to be sensitive to these changes because it was advantageous for human survival. Without being able to notice these changes and act on them, many of our ancestors would have been killed by predators.

In the time since hunter gatherer societies and today, not that much has changed in terms of the human brain. It is still sensitive to the minor changes in our environment, but what happens when those changes simply do not exist? When we spend our days in the same office building, with the same walls and the same equipment and items littered about, we are living in isolation. These environments, while seemingly comfortable for work, can have a devastating effect on the brain if there isn't enough of a break from static. The problem lies with what our brain is expecting versus what it is being fed. Constantly having environments that are static causes the body to go out of balance in terms of when to produce adrenaline. The instinct for fight or flight exists in every person, but the cases of when it is useful has significantly diminished.

The result of our native instincts being placed in our modern environment is that humans often have dramatic reactions to events that do not place us in any real danger. Anxiety goes hand in hand with panic attacks and feelings of helplessness; this is very much the reaction that humans should feel when presented with a life and death situation. The problem is that our modern day events are not life and death; they are solvable problems that simply require a strong will to work through. The fear that one would feels if a large predator suddenly appeared now is invoked in certain individuals when a minor problem arises, such as a large presentation for work. While the presentation itself may be important, it cannot be on the same level of fear as what our ancestors have gone through.

How all of this relates to our anxieties today is simple; our bodies are not used to our modern day qualms and so they produce overreactions to simple problems. While this would be devastating enough, it is not at all the root of our problems. Instead, what many with anxiety suffer from is a result of years of the body becoming acclimated to their environment and producing alarming reactions in the most mundane of events. This is because the human mind is still wired to expect the worst, and so we are constantly on edge.

You may have heard of this idea before. When first presented to me, I was indeed skeptical of how much of this wisdom was relevant in our present day lives. Explaining present day anxiety as it relates to evolution is a satisfying answer, but can it really be correct? I want to stress that there are many factors that create a generalized anxiety disorder, and that this is merely one component to why we feel fear and rushes of adrenaline in the face of minor problems that represent no physical harm. I present this idea first because many of the solutions to treating generalized anxiety come from analyzing this idea and creating situations conducive to how our body expects our environment to be. The tips and advice will come in later chapters, but for now I just wanted to give you a sense of the basis and foundation for how anxiety is analyzed in this book.

A Form of PTSD

In one way or another, every member of modern society is living with some form of Post Traumatic Stress Disorder (PTSD). The first time this idea was presented to me, I thought it alarmist, but as you can see from above, the change in society from forests to cities has created many present day mental health concerns. Humans have not evolved to live in cities, at least not yet. They have not evolved to live static lives that revolve around the same office, the same cafeteria and the same stores. The description of our present day lives would be wholly foreign to our ancestors, and in this comes much of our anxiety.

If you think of modern day anxiety as a form of PTSD, the picture becomes quite clear for what exacerbates this harmful mental state. We are expecting danger, and without an environment that is dynamic and one where we can be on the lookout for predators, our mind has taken to being overactive to minor issues. One must merely take a look at where our anxieties tend to crop up, and put it in perspective of *why* this anxiety is created; you will see that much of our fear is reliant on how our ancestors treated similar situations.

A common cause of my anxiety has been being in social situations where I felt unwelcome. This has nothing to do with whom the actual people were around me, but instead entirely to do with how I *thought* of the people around me. Whether they were coworkers or family, if I felt like a new person to the group my mind would race and I would focus on the minor details of every social engagement. If anxiety is a concern for you, no doubt you have felt the fear and pain of being in a new group. There is concern about saying the right thing, of bringing up the right topic. There is constant anxiety about making a social faux pas. Compounding this issue is that in pleasant society we do not mention to others when they have gone awry, and it is up to the individual to interpret very minor social cues to understand that they have made a mistake. This forces the mind to be ever more vigilant in understanding the actions that one has taken, constantly forcing oneself to analyze their actions and ensure that they have not made a mistake or done something socially unacceptable to the group.

This form of anxiety in the group is a result of our endocrine system being out of sync with our present day lives. It's important to note that there is a fundamental problem, and that our reason for concern is not totally unfounded. It is helpful to be a little bit nervous when in front of a new group, or in front of people in which you are 'unproven'. It instills some fairly important virtues; you are sure to be on your best behavior, and you will be acting to impress and gain acceptance. This is by design, but for those with generalized anxiety, our bodies overact in strong an unpredictable ways. The endocrine system controls the amount of adrenaline released in our body and instead of giving a slight jolt that most others feel, we instead get a large dose that induces panic and causes our severe anxiety.

This is but one form of anxiety, and there are many other cases for how such feelings can manifest. The second and primary method is a worry about the future. Those that suffer with generalized anxiety tend to worry about the future to a greater degree than those not afflicted with the condition. You would think that this would make those with generalized anxiety great planners, but unfortunately fate is not that kind. Instead, what typically happens is the increased level of fear creates a situation of paralysis. A person with anxiety will have a difficult time planning for the future because the chemical reaction in their brain that is supposed to cause a minor amount of worry gets blown out of proportion. In turn the stunned party cannot act and plan for the future. There is too much fear that any one strategy for planning will not be adequate, and so the actions that they take are under constant scrutiny; this scrutiny is self made.

It's incredible that worrying about the future causes so much anxiety in the present, but unfortunately anxiety is a condition that makes us fearful of the future and stunts our ability to act in the present. The constant worry about the future manifests in being wholly unprepared for the present. Though there is thought about the future, the present offers a situation where our brain takes in current events and puts them in the perspective of the future that we are worried about. This is a slightly more complicated idea, but imagine this example: you are at a holiday office party. You know most of your coworkers there but a boss is flying in from out of town. This is your boss's boss, and making a good impression with him or her will have long lasting consequences on how you will move up in the company. The worry about what this social meeting will mean for the future forces the mind to overanalyze the present. Each action that is taken around the boss that you've never met before is magnified. This is made worse because the good actions are never taken with the same amount of significance as the actions that you are worried will make a poor impression. This is a result of looking to the future. By worrying what will come in the future, you are taking the present day events and always creating a worst case scenario for what could happen. No action that you take, even making a good impression, will create a long lasting picture of the future where you are successful. Instead, the mind constantly wanders to picturing how any of your present day actions will cause harm to you or your career in the future.

This status quo of planning for the worst may not seem fair, but again its origins lie in evolution. You just saw an example of how no matter what action is taken at a holiday party, a worker with anxiety will put it in the perspective of a negative action that will affect their future. Imagine now a farmer from centuries ago, far removed from hunter-gatherer society, but not living in our fast paced present. The worry of the future is a net benefit to the farmer; they are able to plan around the seasons and produce a reasonable calendar for harvest. The key difference that I want you to focus on is the possible outcomes for the farmer versus the office worker. The farmer can expect that either the harvest will be good or will be bad. They can almost certainly expect some amount of product from their efforts, and understand the worst case and best case scenarios. The number of outcomes is ultimately fairly limited, and so their fears are put into a perspective that they can plainly see. Our office worker does not have this luxury. They are instead presented with limitless outcomes for what their future in the company will be. Granted it ultimately comes down to whether or not they stay at the company, but how they stay at the company or are forced out come with many different outcomes. The not knowing about the possible outcomes for our office worker is what presents them with a greater level of fear and anxiety than the farmer.

There is a second component beyond outcomes that leaves the farmer in a better position than the office worker. The actions that the farmer takes towards producing a good harvest are ultimately fairly simple. They know what actions to take to produce a good outcome for themself. The office worker does not have it as easy. What will produce the best outcome is a complex set of social interactions and outputted work. It is in no way clear what they need to accomplish in the next six months to have the best possible outcome. This ensures that the fear they have about their future is not in their control.

In essence, this is the anxiety that we feel today. It is a worry of the uncertain future coupled with our inability to know how our present day actions will affect that future. This is a factor of so much of our lives being determined by social hierarchy and social cues. It is much harder to determine the outcomes of social interactions than it is to determine the outcome of the work that a farmer does. For one, the outcomes are limitless and any small action could dictate the future of the office worker. The farmer has a much more narrow set of outcomes, and the work they do can be see in the context of the harvest much more clearly. This is the most common form of our anxiety, and is the base root of our anxiety. Chapters four through six will offer strategies for dealing with this type of anxiety, but before moving on, there is one additional aspect of modern day anxiety I want to focus on; how technology has exacerbated the problems presented by society and our change from nature to the cities.

Information Overload

Static environments, concerns of the future and how our actions determine our future are just some of the factors that contribute to anxiety. In the age of information there is another component that cannot be ignored, the constant flow of information that surrounds us at all times. From the phones in our pockets, to our ever increasing flow of emails, to the constant comparing of one another through social media, technology has improved the ease of our lives at nearly the same rate that it has increased our anxieties.

We are bombarded with information left and right from our waking hours until we sleep at night. There isn't a period greater than sixty seconds where we don't take out our cell phone and look at the trending headlines. We are presented with more information today than at any period in history. While this has been fantastic for learning and creating a more aware society, it has brought with it the problems of too much information. We don't have peaceful moments the way our ancestors did, and without these moments of downtime and total cease of new information, it proves to be too much for our brains. This is half of the information overload problem; our constant reliance on technology to feel connected to the world. It's not about the news stories that we read or the events happening in the world. The problem arises from feeling left out when we are not participating and gaining knowledge and insight into world events. There is a sense of anxiety for some in simply not knowing what the rest of the world is doing. You may have felt this before, a sense that you are missing out by simply not being connected to your phone throughout the day. This is a feeling that persists for many and is the result of training yourself to be constantly occupied and connected through your smart phone.

The second half of anxiety due to technology comes in our constant comparison of one another. This idea will come up with depression, and is more central to that mental health condition, but it is relevant to anxiety as well. By comparing ourselves to our peers, we bring additional stress and worry. Suddenly it is not just our fear about our own lives and where our future is heading, but now we have an unrealistic benchmark to compare ourselves to. Remember that what you see on social media doesn't represent the true lives of our peers. They are instead just snapshots of the high points of their lives. Looking at these high points, it is impossible to compare our ordinary days to the best days that our friends will experience. It produces the feeling that we are both missing out, and that we are slow in accomplishing our dreams. It produces anxiety that we must achieve more, and that we must do it quickly.

Summary

Generalized anxiety disorder is a complicated mental health condition that has numerous factors. It is impossible to discern each and every factor, in particular how they relate to the individual. No two people share the same anxieties, nor are those anxieties of the same magnitude. To get a better hold of anxiety, and to understand how it manifests, one must merely put into perspective our modern lives and how they compare to the lives of hunter-gatherers, as well as farmers. By understanding the slower points in human life, we can see how our bodies have been trained for different conditions than the society that we currently live in. Understanding where our anxieties come from, if only partially, is crucial for understanding how to reduce anxieties' impact on our lives.

Chapter 2: Understanding Depression

A Well Known Enigma

Depression is one of the most common mental illnesses in the world. In the United States alone, there are some fifteen million adults that have been diagnosed with depression. While this number is large, the true number of adults afflicted with depression is likely significantly larger. Depression is a mental disorder that, even for its popularity, is still poorly understood. It is known to be caused by a multitude of factors, some genetic and some lifestyle. Treatment options that are available are immense, and while there are some treatments that are more proven than others, there is no single cure all for depression.

I was diagnosed with depression when I was in college. My diagnosis, like many, was a bittersweet moment. It was nice to put a label on a debilitating aspect of my life and to find treatment, but at the same time the title of depression brings with it a stigma and burden of being classified. Knowing that you have clinical depression means that you are accepting your label and are open to treatment. This is a necessary step for those with depression, but there is an initial period of worry about merely having the label by itself; it is seen sometimes as a character flaw, particularly by the individual with the diagnosis. This is an unfortunate side effect of how society has treated depression over the years. Unlike conditions such as Bipolar disorder, the term 'depression' has many outside uses. These uses have helped color the word over time, and patients see depression as far more than a mental illness. They see it at as something that perhaps they can avoid. They see it as something that everyone goes through, and that it possibly doesn't warrant getting help from a medical professional. While attitudes on this are changing, I want to point out that if you are suffering from depression, you shouldn't feel ashamed. You should try and distance the term 'depression' from the condition of depression. One is a term that has been used for centuries and has taken on a negative connotation that is exercisable by all. The medical term is by far very different, and is something that not everyone experiences. Depression is a lifelong mental disorder and one that needs persistent treatment if it is to be curbed significantly.

Primary Factors

While there are many causes for depression, for the purposes of this book I want to focus on two primary factors: time and comparison. Depression is hard to separate from anxiety, and often a patient will experience both instead of just a single one of these conditions. It should be no surprise that those suffering with depression have difficulty living in the moment; this is exactly the same as those that suffer from generalized anxiety disorder. While those with anxiety tend to focus on the future, patients with depression tend to linger in the past. This focus on their history and their past actions causes the suffering of how they perceive the present and their future. The past consumes their time and so the present becomes a period that is difficult to contemplate. The future becomes almost wholly irrelevant, as a patient will focus so much on the past that they cannot dare plan about their future.

The later chapters have many tips that deal with this first factor of depression, time. If you or a loved one suffer from depression, it should be a major goal to put into perspective the past and to start living in the current moment. You've no doubt noticed that those with depression linger on the past, but it's almost important to note *how* they view the past. Depression is like a lens covered in dust. It takes all moments, good and bad, and makes them murky. It takes moments from the past and adds an air of misery and sadness to events. How often have you thought of your past and put that event in the perspective of what you did wrong? This is something that everyone experiences, but for those with depression, they tend to view all events through this difficult lens. They see all actions that they've done as deciding factors for how they currently feel. This is a difficult condition to treat, and one of the things that can help is reframing the past. We cannot change our past actions, but we can certainly change how we put them into perspective. By looking at our actions and the actions of others that have caused sorrow in the present, we can try and reduce that sadness by softening the overall impact of those actions. The moment that an individual starts to live in the present, and not just the past, is when they start to feel better about themselves. Focusing on the present means that one cannot wallow about the past.

The second major component to depression is in comparison. This too is very similar as to why anxiety can be exacerbated. Depression has always grown stronger when a person with depression compares themselves to their peers. This constant fight within the mind to prove yourself relative to others causes sadness. In our present day it is easier than ever for people to compare themselves to others. Often this comparison is done because of social media. When we read a tweet about our friend's vacation, or when we see their Facebook photos, we can't help but compare our present day situation to the high points of their life. Granted the photos our friend posts do not contain the low points of their trip. It doesn't contain when the kids were complaining on the car ride; it doesn't show the fight a husband got in with his wife. For those with depression, this doesn't matter. They see the high points in the life of their friends and they can only compare how they are feeling to how their friend appears to be feeling in the photos they post online. Even if you don't suffer from major depressive disorder, it is highly likely that you feel a tinge of sadness when you compare yourself to your friend's Facebook feed. This is completely normal and should be expected, but for those with depression this feeling lingers for a much longer period of time. In accordance with treating depression by growing to live in the moment, one needs to separate themselves from their peers. They should be social with their peers, but should not constantly try and compare themselves. You must remember that those with depression do not treat themselves fairly and will always compare themselves in a less than favorable way. The best way to begin the avoidance of this problem is by stopping comparison whenever possible; this is why I strongly advocate removing Facebook if you suffer from depression.

Time and comparison; these are just two factors that I focus on, but know that there are many more. Depression is not just from conditioning, but has shown to be hereditary. The exact percentage of contribution from each factor is unknown, but the treatment is going to be the same regardless of *why* an individual suffers from depression. To treat depression is to embark on a life long battle. It is a fight that you must be vigilante in, but one that can be won with routine, a routine that enforces positive feelings and the value of self worth.

Drug Use and Depression

I have worked with many that suffer from depression. In my time, I have noticed a high correlation between drug use and depression. What came first does not matter, and I don't want to comment on how drug use may cause depression, but rather want to focus on the outcome of using drugs when depressed. Depression has many causes, but the exact mechanical cause in the brain comes down to a chemical imbalance. How this is treated is going to be the same regardless of how this chemical imbalance came to be. That being said, I want to stress that if an individual has been using narcotics to treat their depression, it is a harder road to find stability and happiness. This is because of how drugs affect the brain in the long run, further distorting the chemical imbalance in the brain. I mention this because if you or a loved one use narcotics and suffer from depression, it is paramount to treat a drug addition to also treat depression. You cannot solve one issue without solving the other issue. In addition, understand that it takes longer for those that have abused narcotics to feel good about themselves, the longer it will take to reduce the symptoms of depression. This is not meant to instill a sense of worry in those that have abused narcotics, but I have found that explaining the uphill battle that awaits readies patients for the road ahead. I have seen many that have abused narcotics and overcome their depression, in addition to their drug habit. It can be done, but that individual must prepare themselves and be ready to treat both conditions simultaneously.

Soft Bipolar

Bipolar disorder is a common mental illness. Traditionally there have been two forms of bipolar disorder, identified as Bipolar I and Bipolar II. Bipolar I is categorized as having period of being manic with period of being depressed. Bipolar II however is much similar to depression. It is categorized as having period of hypomania, a light form of mania, with period of extreme depression. In recent times, as of the DSM-V (Diagnostic and Statistics Manual of Mental Disorders, 5th Edition), Bipolar disorder is now thought of as being on a spectrum. There is still a measure of Bipolar I and II, but it is accepted there is a far larger range of how Bipolar affects different people. I mention this here because of the rising idea of 'soft' bipolar. Soft bipolar is extremely similar to depression, so much so that many that have be diagnosed with depression may instead have soft bipolar. The distinction is important because the treatment is quite different. While there are many measures that someone with depression can take to treat their depression, it is much more difficult to treat bipolar disorder without medication.

Soft Bipolar looks so similar to depression because the primary characteristics of the disorder are nearly identical to depression. Soft Bipolar is characterized as by having period of extreme depression mixed with period of 'normal', or a time when depressive characteristics are not as pronounced. This book does not aim to treat or even offer advice for treating soft bipolar, but I realize that readers of this book might suffer from depression. If you believe that the alternating between depressive states and some level of normalcy better describes you than major depressive disorder, I suggest you consult with your doctor. I insert this here merely to bring this disorder to your attention, as it is still fairly new and not well known.

Chapter 3: The Intersection of Anxiety and Depression

The advice in this book is meant to be a practical guide for treating both depression and anxiety. Chapter one and two have helped establish general theories on both disorders, but as you can see they are heavily intertwined. There is more than a strong correlation between the number of people that suffer from depression and anxiety. More importantly, how they suffer is quite similar; both stemming from comparing oneself to others and difficulty in farming the present with the future and the past.

As you continue into the later chapters I want to make very clear that all of the advice in this book is based on my own experiences. That is to say, the advice of the various doctors that I have had over the years, built upon my own experiences and research that I have done. Each method of solving for anxiety and depression have been proven to work, but the degree of effectiveness is highly variable. You may find that a single method is highly effective, or you may find that you need to combine several different methods to reduce your anxiety and depression. It's going to be different for everyone, but it is essential that you never give up. You must stick to a healthy routine to feel better about yourself. Do not waver in your fight against depression and anxiety. Stick to the tips in this book and you will be in a better place than where you started.

Lastly, sticking to a routine when you suffer from depression is very difficult. The mental disorder is categorized by difficulty in finding motivation to participate in life, and ironically this is very much the thing you must do to make yourself feel better. You must make strives to take action before you feel improvement, knowing that improvement in how you feel is a matter of doing these actions first and feeling the result later.

Chapter 4: Things You Can Do Today

Sleep

You know a good night's sleep is important – you've been hearing this all of your life. What you might not know is that sleep is an essential part of combating social anxiety and depression. Poor sleep leads to a body that is unbalanced on a fundamental level. Your adrenaline levels are completely out of sync and your body uses too much effort on activities that should not be stress inducing. You are unable to use your body's energy on the things that matter most, instead wasting your body's energy on negative thoughts that create your anxiety.

So how do we get a good night's sleep? Unfortunately it is easier said than done, and in our ever increasingly technology driven lives, this is only getting more difficult. You will need to create a regimen for yourself, and be diligent – this is something that you will need to follow everyday to see the best results. About an hour or two before bedtime, start preparing for bed. This doesn't mean brushing your teeth at eight at night, but rather you must simply stop working and only engage in relaxing activities. These activities can include watching a movie or listening to music, but you mustn't exercise, answer emails, or spend your evening hours arguing on online forums. About thirty minutes before bedtime you are going to want to cut off all screen time. This means turning off the television, your computer, and your cell phone. This last part is a little bit difficult for some people as our phones have become an essential part of our lives, but that is why we must plan a regimen and know that at thirty minutes before bed, we shut our phone down or agree to not look at the screen and to put all notifications on silent. It's a little effort at first, but chances are the quality of your sleep is not as good as it otherwise could be. Try these tips and it'll be worth the effort for that feeling of waking up relaxed and ready for the day. You'll find your sleep has improved your anxiety through rebalancing your energy levels and reducing your natural stress levels through the release of cortisone in your sleep.

Praise the Sun

You don't need to actually *praise* the sun per-say, but you do need to appreciate its glow. This means going outside and basking in the warm embrace of our star. You need to do this because a deficiency in vitamin D leads to increased levels of stress and anxiety, causing negative feelings. Getting into nature and embracing the warm sun lets our body soak up this beneficial vitamin. Time in the sun has also shown to improve cognitive function and to reduce the levels of depression in many patients.

There is no reason not to follow this easy tip. Some portion of your non-working day involves staring at your phone, reading, or using a portable computer. Take this opportunity to do this activity outside. Your time in the sun does not need to be a sweat inducing event – you simply need to put in the time and enjoy some of the sun's rays, even passively. All it takes is thirty minutes a day and within two to three weeks you should be feeling better and having less anxiety at social events.

Music

I thought it was just me, until I realized that this is common amongst all my friends. After high school and college, so many of us stop listening to music, or do so with far less frequency. We also tend to just listen to what is available, like on the radio or a streaming service. We do not seek out our favorite songs and listen to them repeatedly over the span of several months. Why do we stop doing this? For me personally it was simply a matter of practicality and the number of hours in the day, but listening to music is a simple activity to add into your life that will show benefits for years to come.

Find the music that you enjoy listening to and find a way to obtain that music. You will want to be able to listen to the same few songs whenever you want. This music does not all need to be pop and happy – just listen to the music that you like and what makes you feel good. If you are able to listen to music in a situation that make you nervous, put on that song that you have been hearing for a few months and notice how much better you feel. The thoughts in your head will fade out as memories of activities done while listening to the music will come rushing to mind. You have probably had this experience before – listening to a song and having it take you back to the place and time that you associate with the melody. You want this effect. Music can be like a time machine for your mind and your emotions. Listening to the right song at the wrong time can make all the difference in the world. Try this tip, and even I you can't listen to music in public, you can still enjoy the stress reducing benefits of listening to music on your way home from work or while relaxing before bed.

Arriving on Time

We tend to only remember anxiety as it strikes us in a public place. Whether this is a supermarket trip, a job interview, or meeting a date, we remember the places and associate them with our anxiety because that is when it is at its peak. The truth is that our anxiety starts much before we ever get to the public venue. It usually starts with how we are feeling on the way to our event. People with strong social anxiety tend to be late for events because of their time spent worrying, their time spent thinking through the situation they are about to encounter. What many fail to realize is that the resulting lateness is a key promoter of the stress and anxiety we feel when around other people. Even if it does not matter to the event host that you are late, your mind will still focus on the clock as you are approaching and provide negative thoughts before you ever even enter the social situation.

We can solve this problem by just providing ten or fifteen extra minutes for travel time. This is a very easy solution, but in practice is extremely difficult to implement. We grow into our routines if you are routinely late for events, or simply do not plan enough travel time, adding an extra ten or fifteen minutes is going to be a challenge. The key is to remind yourself that you need this extra time and that this small change will have a large impact on how you feel during a social event. Having the extra time allows us to arrive at a location early, preparing ourselves before we have to go inside and face our company. Remind yourself frequently about the importance of travel time and you will make it a necessary part of your life.

Cleanliness

After a long and stressful day, nothing is worse than coming home to a disorganized mess. This doesn't mean a display like something from *Hoarders*, but rather just a home where you have difficulty finding things, or a place that you would feel uncomfortable showing other people without tidying up first. The feeling of a disorganized home is something that you take with you wherever you go. Our home is part of our identity, and a fundamental part of social anxiety is a worry about who we are. By cleaning our home and making it ready to present to guests, we feel better about ourselves and who we are. We are taking a physical representation of ourselves and giving it the best possible angle at how it looks. In addition, not being able to find what you are looking for is a key part of how anxiety builds in our body. If this is a common occurrence then the buildup can spillover into social situations and make us feel wholly uncomfortable. You must keep a clean home, and with that you will feel better about yourself and not get frustrated by not being able to find items when you need them.

Cleaning is difficult and none of us want to do it, but know the benefits that a clean home brings and you will be more motivated to make your home a comfortable place for you to live, and one where you would love to have guests over and show them around. A tip for how to get started is by taking a survey of your living room, kitchen, and bedroom. This is probably where you spend most of your time and will be the key parts to making your home clean and a relaxing place to spend your time. Do not try and clean your entire home in a single day. Instead, focus on a single room at a time. Breaking down what you need to accomplish into smaller steps is a surefire way to create a feeling of accomplishment. Work on this for a few weeks, or up to a month, and expect to see improved results about how you feel almost immediately. Being able to find what you need when you need it reduces much of the stress created when searching for something frantically right before you need to leave to engage in a social situation. Also, by simply being around your clean home you will feel miles better about yourself. You can take this feeling and bring it out with you into the world and curb your stress.

Frame Your Problems

Not knowing what future events will hold is a leading cause of our anxiety and depression. We can cut down on this feeling by simply making a list of the tasks that we need to accomplish and think about them one by one. This serves a couple of purposes. For one, it helps organize your thoughts into individual pieces. You wont' think about your 'big project' as just a large singular task to accomplish, you will instead think about it as the component parts that you know how to tackle. Breaking down larger tasks in this way makes them less threatening and reinvigorates you to tackle the task. Two, looking at all of the things you need to accomplish frees your mind from having to juggle all of your future tasks. Your mind is partially stressed because it is juggling your calendar and thinking about all of your upcoming events, and also consistently searching for tasks that may have been forgotten as well. It's a simple trick, but the organization of knowing what you need to accomplish really does improve how you think about your tasks at hand. Once you can look at your work as solvable problems, then you will be motivated to take on the tasks and feel less stressed in other situations where you mind wanders to work.

To get started with making to-do lists, start with organizing the simple parts of your life. I suggest starting with a supermarket list and organizing all of the food and items you need. It's a simple start, but you'll notice that if you used to stress mid week about food shopping, that having a list of what is needed helps cut down on this thought process, freeing your mind to focus on other tasks or simply appreciate your free time. You can quickly move on from simple lists about organizing your home to more complicated lists about your work, or even future life goals. Organize the work that needs to be done by your company and break down each task as an easy, medium, or difficult challenge. This helps be realistic about the list and puts into perspective that not every task is identical in difficulty. Work on a set task and return to your checklist to cross off the completed item. This simple action brings a feeling of achievement as you've reached a milestone and know that part of your larger project is complete.

For large goals, goals that can take place in ten or twenty years, make sure that you break these down into extremely granular pieces. Looking at where you want to be in ten years and where you are now can be a real challenge. It can seem like there is no set process you can take to get to where you want to be, but by breaking down the tasks that you need to accomplish you can both be realistic about future goals, and you can organize the small moves you need to make everyday to get to the person that you want to be. Organize your life and start by breaking down simple tasks, and then move onto larger projects and map out all you need to accomplish. Keep that list and cross off completed tasks. If you are ever feeling stressed or worried about upcoming events, simply look at your checklist and note the marked off items. You've started this task, you've worked through some of it already. This thought should ease your tension and help with your anxiety around your coworkers at the office.

Solve One Problem of Yours

If a panic attack feels like it's coming on at work there is a small simple trick you can do to rid this feeling, or at least put it off temporarily. Your anxiety at work comes partially from a fear of failure. You are worried that you might not be able to complete the task at hand, or that when it is turned in your superiors will find the work unacceptable. Even if this is not being processed in your conscious mind, the thought is still buried deep in the depths of your anxiety. You need a way to know that you are capable of solving this project. You need something that can quickly build your confidence and show yourself that you are the right person for the job. This activity also needs to be fun and engaging enough that we can move our mind from worrying to having fun. The best way to solve this larger problem is by solving a simple problem, preferably in the form of a game or puzzle.

Perhaps you already play something like Sudoku, and if you do that's great - you already have a tool at your disposal. The next step is taking this fun distraction and using it when you feel a great burden on your shoulder. If you don't already have a game, I suggest a mentally challenging but complete-able puzzle, something like a Crossword or game of Minesweeper. Games like Tetris and Candy Crush are certainly engaging, but the milestones area a little harder to separate. In Candy Crush much of the progress comes from a randomly generated level that you have no control over – you may just progress out of luck, or get stuck due to randomness. Tetris has a similar problem but is made worse because the game simply isn't that mentally taxing. It has more to do with coordination and we want to find a sense of mental accomplishment. Take your puzzle and complete a few steps of it. This means filling in a few Crossword clues or working part of the way through a Sudoku. Look at the puzzle that you have finished and embrace the feeling of accomplishment. It's a small achievement, but you've shown that you have the mental strength and fortitude to complete a challenging mental task. Now your mind should be ready to take on more challenges as it refocuses on the now and away for the upcoming work that was causing your anxiety and stress at work.

Chapter 5: Things You Can Do Tomorrow

Overload Your Own Senses

The feeling of watching eyes, of thoughts in the room focused on you; the notion that somehow you don't fit in with the room you're in. All of this is caused by an overactive nervous system and an adrenal gland that is not properly separating life and death situations from large rooms with new or uncomfortable groups of people. There are many ways to find short term relief from this effect, but by and far my favorite is with a quick shock to your sense. I recommend this tip only because I tried it, and I was shocked about how effective it was. The goal here is you want to send a surge of real adrenaline to your body, adrenaline caused by the fear of dying. When put back into normal non life threatening events, the feelings of social anxiety and stress are much less pronounced. You will feel more at ease purely because your mind is able to separate out the events that truly require your body's energy, versus the events that you are overreacting to.

There are several ways of sending a shock of adrenaline to your system, but the trick that worked for me was skydiving. This might sound a bit scary, but that is exactly the point of the practice. Skydiving is actually incredibly safe with virtually no fatalities in any given year, but the effect on your brain of jumping out of plane will stay with you for long after the jump. Jump sites can be found outside of most cities, and rates for skydiving are quite reasonable, usually a few hundred dollars a jump. You do not need months of training as a simple course on the day of the jump is all that is required in terms of knowledge. If you decide to go this route, know that you won't be jumping alone, or at least not on your first jump. An instructor will be tethered to you and you will be using his or her parachute to land. You do no need to worry about pulling a lever or making sure your harness is on correctly – the teacher will take care of all of these aspects. All you need to do is fly to Earth, send a shock to your system, and then reap the benefits of reduced stress the next time you are in a social situation.

Skydiving for many people is going to be an immediate turn off. You might have a fear of flying or heights, or you may not have the means to go skydiving at all. There are other ways of pumping your adrenal glands and surging your body with energy. It will take longer but you can do this through exercise, and this is generally recommended for treating all types of anxieties as well. You can also try slightly less shocking events like riding a rollercoaster or a fast moving amusement park ride. You want to give yourself the feeling of a racing heart brought on by something other than social anxiety. Replicating this feeling in other situations reduces the severity of panic when you are in a social environment.

Exercise

It's a simple tip but it certainly isn't easy. Exercise is hard work but it's also been proven to be one of the most, if not flat out the most, effective methods in treating social anxiety and depression. The goal of exercise is to even your body's energy distribution throughout the day, raise your metabolism, and produce endorphins through the build up of muscle. There is no downside to exercise, although it does take time, potentially some equipment, and a location to exercise. To get the best results you will want to focus on both cardio and weight lifting. There is a positive correlation in both those that run more, and those that increase muscle mass, and a decrease in their levels of generalized anxiety. This extends to all types of fitness and exercise, and at a very minimum, your improved body will make you feel better about your self and enhance your body image.

To get started you will first want to create a schedule. It's a step a lot of people overlook, but it's an essential part of ensuring that you exercise consistently and are realistic about your muscle and weight goals. Try and just focus on three times a week. Plan it around days that you know are free, and do not plan on waking up earlier or staying up later to exercise. You want to work your exercise into your existing schedule. Try and find a fun activity to participate in and this will improve your chances of sticking to an exercise plan. This might include joining a local soccer team, or meeting some friends for a game of Frisbee. You are likely nervous about joining another group due to anxiety, and so remember that a gym, or even your own home, are perfectly suitable substitutes.

For a cardio workout, I recommend getting twenty to thirty minutes of heavy breathing and an increase in your core body temperature. We are working out purely to sweat when it comes to cardio. You want to get your heart rate high and maintain that level for fifteen to twenty minutes. This increased heart level will translate to a more relaxed heart when in difficult social situations. Your enhanced cardiovascular system will significantly reduce the physical effects you feel from stress. This includes things like sweating or getting red in the face and extremities. If you aren't in condition to go running, or get your heart beat appropriately high, that's perfectly fine. Start with walking and work your way up from there. Even if you never move past walking you will still be at a significant advantage to where you were before. The effects will be less pronounced, but you should notice a decrease in all physical symptoms brought on from social anxiety.

Weight lifting is slightly easier proposition, but it is needed in conjunction with a good cardio workout. Weightlifting will tear the muscle fibers in your body, replacing them with stronger fibers and making you more buff and create a lean desirable definition. The real benefit comes in our brain's response to weight lifting where endorphins flow because we are gaining muscle. The endorphins sent out improve our mood and reduce our stress. This effect is long lasting and will carry itself to your workplace. There are many different weight lifting techniques, but you should be doing them about ten minutes of lifting three to four times a week. You can do these on the same days as your cardio workout, or you can do them on separate days. If you do not have the proper equipment for weight lifting, that is no problem. Simply use your body's existing weight and focus on exercises like crunches, sit-ups, and pushups. It's a small time investment for a long lasting benefit that will make you feel better about yourself and improve your self-image to ease your anxiety during social situations.

Feel Great from a Great Diet

A fundamental change to your diet is required if you want to rid yourself of depression and anxiety. It's a long form step and will take many months to see the true benefits of changing one's diet, but don't fret, there is one step that you can do today to alleviate some of the stress you might currently have.

Food is an essential part of our culture and our history. When feeling down or depressed after a long day, or even when out at a social function where food is being served, one of the best things we can do is simply eat a good comfort food. Comfort food is going to be different for every individual and be even more different across cultures. Take a moment to enjoy a meal that you truly love, something that remind you of home and brings on feelings of love and care. For me personally, that means eating a good meatloaf dinner with mashed potatoes, peas, and gravy. It's not a health conscious move, that's for sure, but that doesn't make me feel any less better when I'm done eating. The aim in comfort foods is not for nutrition or health, but rather just to get a sense of the safety and security that we felt when we were younger. Even if right now isn't a time that you need to munch on a security food, you should still map out the restaurants and grocery stores around you where you can find some comfort food. Think about what food your family used to eat when you were younger and try and bring this feeling back to life. Don't worry about the cost too much either – this isn't something you should be doing very often. There is a chance that comfort food makes you feel worse, it just remind you of home and brings you deeper into a stupor, and in this case you already know that you should avoid comfort food. If this describes you, or even if you find success with comfort food, there is another aspect of our health identified with food, and that's our general diet.

A dietary shift is hard, especially if we are moving from a mostly innutritious diet to a healthy nutritious one. Comfort food aside, so much of the food that is boxed or frozen is loaded with salt, fats, and needless preservatives. This gunk might make you feel better in the short term, but in the long term it weakens your immune system, causes weight gain, and can leave you feeling out of energy and tired just shortly after completing a meal. You instead need to focus on nutritious healthy foods that will leave you feeling energized and fresh. To change your diet on such a basic level, you're going to need to make some hard changes. For one, identify your current diet and figure out the trouble spots. There are invariably some meals that you have that have little to no nutritional value. We want to axe these in favor of more nutritious and fresh foods. Find a simple cookbook and work with the recipes within to find the foods that you like and are easy to make. We live in a time where many cookbooks cater to those that have limited time and are not necessarily knowledgeable about the various vegetables and spices we need. These books have easy recipes that can frequently be completed in less than thirty minutes. Use this as a guide and mix it with other recipes of foods from different regions. The recipes are important, but they are only as helpful as the quality of the ingredients.

A change to a healthier diet does not need to be an expensive shift. When people think of quality ingredients they think of the expensive organic foods at their local supermarket. I want you to know that you do not need to eat organic to eat healthy. Organic foods commonly carry just as many pesticides as foods that are not labeled organic. Focus on the quality of the fruits and vegetables you buy based on look and feel, and never worry about the label. For meats, poultry and fish, buy from your local butcher at your supermarket. Never buy the precut meats as these are never as good as the ones cut right in front of you. Your butcher has to see your face when he hands you your product – this just isn't the case with those that are selling you meats that are prepackaged. Once you have the foods you are going to prepare and the recipes you are going to use, you can start to focus on the joy of cooking.

There is something essential, Earthly even, to cooking. There is a strong connection between what you are putting in your body and how you feel. Knowing that the food in your stomach was selected and prepared by you will have an immediate positive effect. You can literally see these benefits within two to three days. At work or at a social situation you will feel better as you know that your body is filled with foods that it needs, and not unwanted and unnecessary chemicals and preservatives. There is also simply the act of cooking itself. It is a relaxing experience in the evening and you can melt away the day's stresses by preparing your food and embracing the feelings and sensations that come from cutting, dicing, and washing your food. Eating comfort food is an absolutely great way to feel better immediately, but refining your diet over time will have life long benefits affecting everything from health to the way you feel around others.

Chapter 6: Looking to Your Future

Consider Finding a Professional to Talk To

Communication and therapy can be a vital part to improving your anxiety and depression. This is a step that many sufferers of these disorders simply to not wish to partake in. Finding a therapist should not be a scary situation, but you should know that it is time consuming and could potentially be cost prohibitive. Provided you have the option, pure therapy is recommended before turning to medications. The advantage of a therapist is that they help delve into your underlying problems. You might find that your social anxiety is simply a point on part of spectrum of a larger problem. I myself have never found a therapist that I truly liked, however I have had friends that found wonderful therapists and that helped them through all sort of difficulties in their lives. I see the potential benefit to a therapist as a huge plus, but the first few steps that you have to take to finding one are harder than they need to be.

If you've decided that you'd like to find a therapist, your first step is going to be looking at your finances and your health insurance plan. As part of the Obama-Care act of 2012, mental health services are a required feature of all plans that are featured on the exchange. This almost always means that you have an option to find a therapist and go to a few appointments and your insurance company will cover the cost. There are many therapists that operate out of network and will not be covered on any insurance policy. You can expect these therapists to have a stronger pedigree than many that would be covered by insurance, and you can also expect that they cost a decent chunk of change more. From my experience of searching, I found that sessions could range anywhere from $200 to $500, and that a session was typically defined as somewhere between thirty minutes and an hour. This is quite the price to pay, but depending on your financial situation you may find that these top tier of therapists are right for you. If your finances dictate that you cannot see someone that charges so much, you have no reason to fear, a large part of the therapy process is simply talking through your problems, and it doesn't matter so much who is on the other side receiving the information. To find a more moderately priced therapist, go to your healthcare provider's website and do a doctor lookup for 'behavioral care'. Part of the reason that many people do not move beyond this step is because there is no lookup for a 'therapist' – the name will always be listed as 'behavioral care' or some other similar description. Make sure that you find doctors that are not listed as psychiatrists. A psychiatrist will always turn to prescription medicine to aid in solving a problem, whereas a therapist will always talk the problem through with you. Once you have found a doctor near you, check with your insurance policy to see what your co pay for secessions will be, as well as how many secessions you have before you have to pay out of pocket. When I first started looking for therapist, I was surprised to find that my health insurance would only pay for ten appointments, and any session after this would be hundreds of dollars. If your insurance policy looks something similar to the way that mine did, then I suggest that you look to a different method of therapy. You will have to rely on your friends and family to speak through your problems, but don't worry, there are steps for that situation as well.

You will know that you have found a good person to talk to when they can just sit and listen, and all of this without you feeling as though they are being judgmental. It's important to share your experiences with others – this is one of the key advantages of finding a significant other. The advice that they give is not as important as the fact that they are understanding of your personal struggle. You want to make sure that every word that you say to them is being registered and that they do not zone out, or give you the feeling they are not paying attention. Knowing that another person is listening to your problems brings a sense of unity with others, a sense that your struggles are not unique, but in fact something that we all deal with, simply on a different scale. Finding someone to talk to is scary – you are sharing your life experiences with this person and asking for advice on very personal situations, but follow the steps above and you will find someone that can help you and make you feel less anxious in crowds.

Consider Medication

It's a discussion that you must ultimately have with your doctor, but depending on how long you've lived with your depression and anxiety, it might be time to look at medications. I want to give you a brief overview of some of your options in case you decide to talk to a doctor. I myself have two medications, one that I take daily for depression and one that I *can* take for anxiety. I have found the other tips in this book to be enough of a booster that I don't need my anti-anxiety medication, but if things got truly unbearable I could take it, and from past experiences I know that it truly does work.

You must keep in mind that treating anxiety with medication is unlike treating other mental ailments. Usually there is something coupled with social anxiety, like depression or a generalized anxiety disorder. In cases of a persistent model of irregular thought processes, a doctor will likely recommend an anti-depressant. Antidepressants do more than just treat depression; they can ease your anxiety over time. The range in price, side effects and primary effects of antidepressants is wide and varied. If you feel like social anxiety is your sole issue, I would not recommend taking stronger, more expensive non-generic antidepressants. The side effects and price probably aren't worth the possible benefits. For most suffering from depression, common antidepressants that have been on the market for years tend to be highly effective. They are proven drugs that are among the safest on the market, due to their extensive testing and begin in use for decades.

For treating rapid onset anxiety, there are a few drugs that are commonly prescribed. Not quite as common as antidepressants, Xanax or the generic equivalent works to relieve all types of anxiety very quickly. This is the drug that I have access to but rarely ever take. As I said I found success with these other tips and have not needed to rely on this powerful relaxer, however it is just that, it does relax and it is extremely powerful. I would describe it as having one to three alcoholic drinks, depending on dosage, in rapid succession. The feeling is slightly different than alcohol in that you are a little bit more alert and you won't be slurring your speech, unless at very high doses. The main problem with these types of drugs, Xanax or others in the benzodiazepine family, is that they are habit forming, lose effectiveness over time, and will almost never be prescribed for daily intake for a period longer than thirty days. If your anxiety is truly life debilitating, there is a chance that your doctor will recommend taking Xanax everyday, but even in these cases such a treatment plan does not exceed thirty days. The reason is that all of these types of rapid acting drugs are extremely addictive, both physically and mentally. Taking them for long period of time can also cause a variety of respiratory problems and other health issues.

I hope that you are able to use the other tips in this book to resolve your anxiety and depression, but if you do take the medication route, it's important to weigh your options. Think through what a treatment means and whether or not you want your anxiety to be dependent on a drug. Most importantly, if you do decide to take drugs, speak with your doctor and work through an appropriate regimen that fits you.

Conclusion

Thank you again for downloading *Cognitive Behavioral Therapy: The Definitive Guide to Understanding Your Brain, Depression, Anxiety and How to Overcome It.*

Anxiety and depression are life long illnesses. They are can be hard to detect, and often go unnoticed for years. Once they have developed, they are can be very hard to treat. Making the issue more complicated, treatment is going to be slightly different for each and every individual. You now have a knowledgebase of information about anxiety and depression. You have generalized theories for why depression and anxiety are so common in modern society, and you have a toolbox to refer to treat these illnesses.

There is no shame to having anxiety or depression. They are conditions that are not the fault of our actions; there is nothing that we could have done to prevent these illnesses. I have that you take the suggestions in this book to heart. All of the tips that I have provided have greatly helped me. Today, I feel better at work and am more relaxed in social situations. The advice in this book may work, but remember that is not an instantaneous result. You will need to work hard to remove anxiety and depression from your life, and realistically the best we can ever hope for is to minimize complications caused by anxiety and depression.

Use the advice in chapters four and five. Most of what I have provided are actions that you can take yourself. Remember that anxiety and depression might not be something you can tackle by yourself. If you feel that you need the help of others, seek aid in the form of a therapist or psychiatrist. I highly recommend speaking to a therapist before moving to a psychiatrist. A therapist will seek to solve your problems through communication, whereas a psychiatrist will more than likely want to offer medication. In the end, if medication is what it takes, do not feel afraid to take medicine to treat these conditions; millions of Americans have found success through medication, myself included.

Thank you and good luck!

Book – IV

Cognitive Behavioral Therapy Mastery

How to Master Your Brain and Your Emotions to Overcome Depression, Anxiety and Phobias

Introduction

Congratulations on downloading this book and thank you for doing so.

The following chapters will discuss simple strategies that you can use to become a true master at cognitive behavioral therapy, one of the most commonly used techniques in the treatment of anxiety, depression, and phobias.

There are plenty of books on this subject on the market, thanks again for choosing this one! Every effort was made to ensure it is full of as much useful information as possible, please enjoy!

Chapter 1: A Brief Look at cognitive behavioral therapy

To be able to truly master cognitive behavioral therapy and all of the techniques that come with it, you need to first understand how the brain works, what anxiety or depression can do to it and how cognitive behavioral therapy is actually able to help your brain. To get the most use out of this book, it is a good idea to read *Cognitive Behavioral Therapy: The Definitive Guide to Understanding Your Brain, Depression, Anxiety and How to Overcome It*. That is the first book in this series and will give you *all* of the basics that you need to know to be able to get started on truly becoming a master of your anxiety and the cognitive behavioral therapy that will help you to become a happier, healthier person.

While you should have learned most of what you need to know about the way that anxiety and depression can affect your brain in the last book, this chapter is going to serve as a refresher course on the way that they work and the way that cognitive behavioral therapy is able to help you with each of them.

Anxiety and depression are both closely related and are often the result of a misfire or an action that was inappropriate for the situation. For example, someone may experience anxiety because they had a surge of adrenaline driving their vehicle to the store two miles down the road. They would then begin to associate driving with adrenaline. The fight or flight response would kick in each time that they got behind the wheel of a car and they would feel that their life was being threatened. It could then escalate to an extreme point, and that is the way that anxiety works. It tricks the brain into thinking that normal situations are dangerous. This fight or flight response is a leftover mechanism from the days when humans *did* need to either run (from a predator) or prepare to fight (that same predator). While most people do not need to run up a tree to get away from a bear or prepare to kill it with their spears, the surge of adrenaline will still come from normal situations, and it is something that people need to overcome.

The same principles work with depression without the Paleolithic feel attached to it. Humans are designed to feel emotions. Sadness is one of the most extreme emotions that a person can feel and the brain will sometimes get caught in a loop and tell someone to continuously feel sad. This can be triggered by anything – from a change in physical status to a new job to even...anxiety! The brain will tell the person that he or she needs to become sad for reasons that would normally be considered "every day" and the person would get stuck there. That is the way that depression works in the brain.

cognitive behavioral therapy works to combat both of these in the way that it deals with the brain. The point of cognitive behavioral therapy is to trick the brain into getting into a new pattern and retrain it how to think like a "normal" brain. Cognitive behavioral therapy is as simple as a training method that will teach a person by retraining their brain to think in a way that makes sense. When a person goes through cognitive behavioral therapy, it can sometimes be uncomfortable physically, but more commonly it is uncomfortable emotionally.

The good news is that cognitive behavioral therapy is *very* effective at treating anxiety, depression, and phobias. It has been proven to be one of the best ways to combat the problems that come with each of these disorders, and it is actually one of the fastest ways to normalize the brain. cognitive behavioral therapy is not one standalone method but a combination of many different things that will allow you to overcome the problems that your brain has. Each of these methods has been proven to work and have slightly different approaches but will be able to accomplish the same thing – overcoming anxiety, depression or phobias.

A word of caution: not all mental disorders are able to be treated with cognitive behavioral therapy, and you should first get the clearance of a medical professional before you try to start any type of behavioral therapy on your own. Be sure that you have anxiety, depression or phobias before you start cognitive behavioral therapy because these problems can mimic other mental disorders. It is always best to follow the advice of your physician and continue taking any medication that has been prescribed to you if you have a mental disorder. Starting a program, stopping medication or trying to "fix" yourself without the approval of a doctor can be detrimental to your health.

Chapter 2: Multimodal Therapy

One of the most comprehensive ways that people can use cognitive behavioral therapy is through Multimodal therapy. This is a type of therapy that utilizes several different avenues to allow people to see the different ways that they are affected by their anxiety and depression. Once they figure out how their anxiety or depression shapes each of these areas of their lives, they can begin working on the healing process and making sure that they are able to overcome the problems that they have. Multimodal is the way that a person's behavior, affects, sensations, images, cognition, interpersonal relationships, and dependence are all affected by anxiety or depression.

Behavior

The behavior that is seen in people who have anxiety and/or depression is different depending on what they are dealing with and to what degree. It is important to note that there are many different behavior problems that can come from both anxiety and depression. These include:

- Childish acts
- Inappropriate acts
- Extreme obedience
- Destructive behavior
- Compulsive behavior
- High levels of self-control

While all of these behaviors are not uncommon to see in people who are not dealing with anxiety and depression, they can be exacerbated by the disorders. The main characteristic of this is that the behaviors are negative and can cause serious problems for the person who is doing the behaviors.

The multimodal way of treating these behaviors is to figure out what they are and directly address them to figure out what type of problems they could be causing as a secondary result of the disorders that are affecting the brain.

Affects

There is always a way that anxiety and depression can affect a person but when dealing with a multimodal type of treatment, the effect is the intensity of which emotions are felt, and actions are done. A person who has anxiety may have a much more intense effect than someone who has depression, and it can be a problem in both instances.

In general, someone who does not have a mental disorder would not generally feel very strong emotions. The emotions that people who have anxiety and depression feel are actually what can cause them to seek out therapy in the first place – they may be concerned that their emotions are out of control.

It is important to note that just recognizing these emotions and even, in some instances, talking about them, will not be able to change the way that they are in the brain. It is something that takes several levels of therapy to get to and can sometimes take a longer time to be able to address it. There are different emotions that are associated with the intensity, and that can change the way that the person who has anxiety or depression does things.

Sensations

These are the physical symptoms that are felt during a bout of anxiety or depression. The most common are:

- Sweating
- Tension
- Physical pain
- Nausea
- Increased heart rate
- Shaking
- Fidgeting

These are common during an anxiety attack or even during a dark time while someone is depressed. They can affect the way that a person does things and it can be harder for a person to concentrate when these physical symptoms are going on.

The multimodal aspect of this is that one of the other things that are happening – like images or cognition – can cause each of these physical symptoms to manifest. Sometimes, though, there are problems and a person may feel these for no reason at all. They may not know it, but there could have been something that did actually trigger them to feel these feelings.

It is important to note that the sensations are not going to be fixed by fighting them. The person who feels the sensations should accept them for what they are because trying to fight them can actually make them worse. By acceptance, a person will be able to start the healing process that goes along with the therapy.

Images

People who have anxiety and depression are often able to see the worst possible scenario of a situation. This is imagery by which they associate nearly everything with, and it can be a problem or a benefit. If someone is constantly thinking about the worst case scenario, they may avoid doing simple things like driving or going to the store. This leads to even higher anxiety and depression levels for that person.

The way in which images can be the *good* thing is that once someone learns to channel the imagery in their mind and turn it into a positive thing, it can help them to solve problems. It is not uncommon for creative people to be depressed or have anxiety because of the bold images that they often see.

Cognition

Self-talk and the inner voice are the easiest ways to understand cognition in any person. A person with anxiety or depression will often use negative self-talk, and they will have an inner voice that is not very strong. They may struggle with the thoughts that they do have or even their opinions of themselves.

When using multimodal therapy, the point is to try to replace the negative cognition with positive. This is done through various methods including using images to make things more positive for the person who is experiencing negative self-talk.

Interpersonal

There are many relationships issues that people may experience when they have anxiety or depression. It is something that can have a negative effect on the way that things are done and the way that they interact. With multimodal therapy, a person can change their interpersonal relationships by learning how to cope with things in a healthy way instead of being codependent to another person.

Dependence

When it comes to people who have anxiety or depression, there is a higher chance that they will have dependencies on chemicals or emotions. It can affect the way a person chooses to do things, but it can be different depending on the way that a person functions. Whether they are able to sleep, use drugs or even depend on another person will all be related to the anxiety and depression. Multimodal therapy can change this by creating different cognitive patterns and negative associations with the dependency items. It is something that will change the way that the person is able to function and make them better able to deal with things without reaching for something that they had previously been dependent on.

The main idea of multimodal therapy is to combine each of the different aspects of negative thinking and negative behaviors and replace them with positive things. It is important that the person doing this do it in *all* areas and pay close attention to the way that each of the different aspects is connected to each other.

Chapter 3: Looking at Reality

Trying to adjust to a reality that isn't ideal can be difficult for some people, but it is something that needs to be done to be able to overcome anxiety and depression. People who are able to overcome it are those who want to make sure that they are doing the right thing and that they are not the victim of their past. By looking at the past and overcoming it, reality therapy is able to change the way that the present is handled. People who choose to overcome it will no longer be victims of their past but will, instead, be able to flourish in their new role as someone who has defeated an anxiety or depression disorder.

Right and Wrong

The first thing that reality therapy will focus on is whether or not something is right or wrong. The therapy aims to take a look at the way that things can change and the different aspects of it. The person should decide whether something is right or wrong.

When using reality therapy, the person needs to listen to their own inner voice. Most are surprised to find that it is difficult to think of what *they* believe instead of what they have been told to believe or what they have been told is right or wrong. This is something that will change the way that they do things, though, and it will give them a better chance at doing more for themselves. When they are able to use their own inner voice instead of the voice of someone else who has told them how to think, they will be able to make a decision on what is right and what is wrong.

The easiest way to do this is to create a list of things that are in the moral gray area. The list can be anything that is close to them or related to them, but it should be something that has strong moral implications. When the person looks at it, they should decide the black and white area that the previously gray area item went into. It is something that will change depending on the situation, and it will give them a new perspective on the way that they should feel about things instead of just going off of whatever they have been told to feel.

Responsibility

When a person experiences anxiety or depression, they may feel like they can place the blame on something or someone else. The biggest thing that they need to be able to do is learn how to take responsibility for their own mental illness. It can be difficult, but it is something that can be done with a little bit of practice.

To be able to take responsibility of their mental disorder, they need to look at the *whys* of having it. Do they think that they have it from their parents? Because they had a traumatic youth? Because they don't know how to function in social situations? By looking at each of these reasons, it is clear to see that they are putting the blame on something other than themselves.

It can be really difficult to get to this point, but it is a good thing once it happens. If a person is able to look at themselves and say: "I have depression as a result of my own brain reacting differently" they will then be able to take care of the problem and make sure that they are fixing their depression.

The difference in responsibility and blame is that a person who is responsible for something aims to fix the problem that is currently happening. A person who is blaming someone for their problems will not want to fix the current problem but will, instead, be focused on the problems of their past. They will want to blame these people for the problems that they have.

Realism

Understanding the way that the world works is one of the most important qualities that come along with trying to make reality therapy work. The person who has anxiety or depression may be stuck in the past in their own head, and that is something that can be a problem. By taking a step back and looking at the different things that can be done in the present, they are going to give themselves a better chance at reality. It is a great way for people to make sure that they are getting the most out of reality and that they are able to provide themselves with the best opportunity possible.

The easiest way to do this is to keep track of each of the things that are actually going on. A person should write down the different positive things that are happening in their daily lives. By keeping track of this, they can, essentially, pull themselves out from the muck that is in the past and can be holding them down. It is a good idea to make sure that the things they are focusing on, in reality, are positive.

By making sure that they know what is going on with reality and that things are happening all around them, they will have a better chance at moving on from the past, doing the right thing and joining everyone in reality.

Overcoming It

Each of these methods can make reality therapy truly work for anyone who is suffering from anxiety or depression. It is one of the easiest therapy options regarding logistics, but it can be hard for people to make sure that they are truly pulling themselves out of the past. Because of the problems that come with the different therapy methods, people may want to choose reality as a way to make sure that they are doing things the right way.

While it may be uncomfortable to focus on the present instead of the past, it is one of the first steps of healing. With reality therapy, people can make sure that they are getting the most out of each situation and that they are doing the best job possible at becoming a better, happier person.

Reality therapy does not always work the way that you want it to. It may take some extra time and may be a problem for people who are in different situations. It can be extremely detrimental for people to think that they are going to be able to do different things in a world that is truly real, instead of thinking about the different ways that they will not be able to do things. Because of this, a person should always be cautious when they are using reality therapy. It can be painful to look at the past and overcome it, but it can also be beneficial for people who want to be able to do more with the past and with the different things that they have going on at the present time.

Chapter 4: Acceptance and Commitment

Unlike many of the other cognitive behavioral therapy techniques that you will learn throughout the course, acceptance and commitment therapy does not get rid of the negative thoughts that you have. Instead, it focuses on accepting the thoughts and learning to manage them through commitment. There are two different approaches that people can take when they are using the acceptance and commitment technique to overcome anxiety and depression. The two techniques that are used are FEAR and ACT which are acronyms that stand for different steps that you can take.

Fuse Your Thoughts

This is where you are going to stop your thoughts from "running." If you have thoughts that will not stop and are just going around in circles, you need to fuse them together to make sure that you are able to stop them. By fusing your thoughts, you are going to slow down the thinking process which can put a halt on the fight or flight response. It is a way to make sure that you are getting the most out of the situation and it will allow you the chance to make sure that you can take a step back to do the next part of the process.

Expand on What Has Happened

Take an outside look at everything that is going on. Did you get in the car to drive and started having physical symptoms? Did you try to do something normal and it turned into a big production? Were you uncomfortable in a social situation? By taking a look at what has happened, you will allow yourself the chance to expand on the experience and what is going on. You will make yourself objective to the situation instead of passive where the situation is affecting you. Expand on what you know about the experience and what you are doing with the experience. Try to figure out the rational explanation for the experience and the way that it is going to happen to you.

When you are struggling with anxiety or depression, this can be one of the hardest things that you will need to do. It will also be the most helpful to you during this time, and you can make sure that you are getting the most out of the experience by expanding on it.

Avoid Your Senses

When you are struggling with depression or an anxiety attack, your senses are going to be reacting to the fight or flight system in your body. They are going to be doing different things that you may not understand. During these times, it is best to avoid your senses. Do not pay attention to the fact that your fingers feel like they are tingling, that you have bad taste in your mouth or that your sixth sense just feels off. It is your brain trying to trick you.

Instead of focusing on your senses, you can avoid your senses by trying to focus on different actions. Pay attention to the actions that you are doing and what is going on around you. Do not run away from your senses but, instead, put them on the back burner and try to make sure that they are not interrupting what you need to get done.

Reframe Your Situation

This in no way means that you need to run from the situation or change it to do something else. You need to only look at it in a different light. Spin it so that it is positive. If you have to give a big presentation at work and your anxiety is getting the best of you, think of it in a positive way. At least you have work to give a presentation at, and nearly everyone has done it before so it can't be that bad.

The reframing process can be hard, but it will give you a chance to make sure that you are getting the most out of the situation. It will also teach you how to look at things more objectively instead of just running from things that might be going on while you are having anxiety or you are depressed.

Accept and Focus

The first part of the ACT plan is to accept the emotions that you are having no matter how negative they are. Think about them as thoughts that are coming to your head and let them flow through it. Allow them the space to give you some worry. By accepting that something bad *could* happen, you will give yourself the chance to make things actually happen in your life. It will also give you the chance to do more with what you are planning. Accepting negative thoughts causes them to lose their power within your own mind.

Once you have accepted the thoughts, focus on them and what the worst case scenario would be. What would be so bad if you did mess up the presentation? What would be the problem if you *did* have an anxiety attack while driving? Each of these things is truly not that bad and can make a difference in your life depending on the different things that you have going through your mind.

Create Your Plan

Decide what you are going to do with the thoughts that you just accepted. Are you going to take them and act on them by not driving or not doing the presentation? Are you going to make it harder to think about the different situations that you could be in? Are you going to ask the thoughts to leave?

Having a plan in place for negative thoughts is the only way that you will be able to overcome them. Make sure that you know what you want to do with them and where you want them to go. Give yourself time to plan your negative thoughts *before* they happen so that you will be prepared. Handle the thoughts according to what you want your actions to be and what you want to be able to overcome. This will give you a chance at making sure that you can get over the negative thoughts and that you can make your life a better one.

Time to Act

Once you have accepted the negative thoughts as normal and something that will just always be there and you have made the plan that you wanted to be able to put into place, you can then act on that plan. Make sure that you know what is going on and what you are going to be able to do with your negative thoughts. Each of these thoughts will make things harder for you but having the plan in place will give you an opportunity to act.

If you deliberately do this for each of the negative thoughts that you have, you will eventually learn how to do it automatically. This is a coping method and something that can be used very easily once you have an idea of how to do it. You will be able to retrain your brain so that it automatically accepts all of your negative thoughts, uses the plans that you have put into place and acts on the plans that are there. It will allow you to overcome the negative thoughts just by accepting them.

Chapter 5: Functional Analytics

The functional analytic form of cognitive behavioral therapy focuses on noticing the way that someone does something, looking at the way that the person responds and changing the way that they respond to it. This is something that can change depending on the situation and will make things better for the person who is undergoing the therapy. This method is difficult to use on your own, but it can be done with someone else who can look at the way that you do things.

Negative

When a person has a negative response to something, that is what needs to be noticed, accepted and changed. This can be a negative result to anything from having to get up to work to driving their car to talk in front of people. The person who is helping out with this type of therapy needs to figure out what brings negative emotions to the person who is undergoing the therapy. This will allow him or her to make sure that things are done in a controlled environment.

The helper should then give the person an idea of something that will bring about the negative behaviors. This can be something as simple as saying, "I can't help you anymore" to "You have to drive 1,200 miles, you have no choice." The negative response will then kick in, and the person who is receiving the therapy may light up in different areas physically. They will also have an emotional response but it is a good idea to focus only on the physical since that is something that will be much easier for them to change the way that they do things when something negative happens to them or in any other situation that they may be in that could cause them to feel anxiety or become depressed.

Positive

The opposite works for things that are positive for the person. The helper should tell the person who is receiving therapy something that is positive like "I bought you some flowers for no reason" or "You have an extra 100 dollars in your checking account." This will also cause the person to light up physically. They will be able to then notice the changes that their body goes through when they are doing different things, and it will give them the chance to see that they do have the capability to have a positive attitude.

The helper needs to encourage this behavior for the person to be able to truly see that it is making a difference. When the helper praises the person for having a positive reaction, it will show the person that things can get better and that they are able to enjoy things. This is an especially helpful technique for people who are depressed or who are going through a particularly bad bout of anxiety.

When the helper shows them that they are capable of positive behavior and encouraging it, they will show them that things can get better and that they will be able to apply this to different situations. The more positive a person is, the better able they are to track their physical reaction to positive things.

Bringing Change

The biggest change that should occur is that the person works on the physical symptoms when there is something that is negative going on with the different things that they have. When a person clenches their teeth or scrunches up their eyebrows in response to being told that they are going to have to do one more work assignment, they will be able to see that they are reacting physically. It is something that needs to change, though, and once they are able to see what they are doing and how they are reacting to the different negative situations, they can start to change.

The change needs to happen by first getting back to a neutral place. When the person notices that they are reacting, they can take a pause and bring themselves back down to the way that things are going. It is something that will make them better able to react to these situations and will allow them the chance to make sure that they are not reacting in a physical sense.

By noticing and overcoming each of these things, a person will be able to make sure that they are able to overcome the emotional problems. The first thing that usually happens is physical, and the subsequent actions are usually emotional. Once you overcome the physical part of reacting to a situation, you will then be able to overcome the emotional part of the different things that are going on.

Praise

The praise part is just as important in the negative areas as it is in the positive areas. The person who is helping out should always make sure that he or she is encouraging the person who is able to drop back down to neutral when they experience the negative emotion. This is something that will need to make things better and will allow them to see that they are doing things the right way. It is a way to show them that their behavior can be changed and that they are capable of making their own lives better without the help of nonsense.

When the helper notices that the physical reaction is gone, he or she should try their hardest to show the person who is undergoing the therapy that they are going to be able to continue doing that. By telling them "good job" or showing them that things will get better, they will be able to make sure that they are doing things the right way and that they are getting the most out of the experience.

It is a good idea to notice the way that a person is encouraged once they are praised. If they receive enough praise when they do something positive and again when they are able to drop back down to neutral, they will associate the neutral position with something that is positive. It will be a good way for them to change the way that they do things without ever even having to try.

Keeping it Up

Once a person has learned what they are able to do with their positive attitude and the praise that comes along with doing things the right way, they will be able to continue that behavior. While it may seem like they are only teaching themselves how to do something the right way, they are actually showing their brain how it should be reacting to different situations.

The brain is a powerful thing that people with anxiety and depression need to overcome. While it can be helpful, it can also be detrimental. If you constantly bring praise and teach yourself the right way to react to different stimuli, even normal things, you can show your brain what it is supposed to be doing. The trick is to make it think that it is doing the right thing and that will, in turn, make the manifestation that comes about in your own physical symptoms the correct way that they are supposed to be.

Chapter 6: Cognitive Processing

The way to which the mind responds to an event or other stimuli is powerful and can cause a person to become "set in their ways" with their ability to do different things. Because of this, cognitive processing therapy is sometimes used to change the way that a person thinks of a certain situation, feeling or even a past event. It is an effective cognitive therapy technique, and it allows the person to overcome the problems that they had in the past. The first part of healing an anxiety or depressive disorder is to move forward from things that have happened in the past and that have been detrimental to the person.

Learning About It

To be able to successfully learn the right way to overcome the problems that a person has with anxiety or depression, they must first look at the past. They need to see what type of problems they had in the past, the way that their problems affected them and how they shaped them for the future of everything that they are going to be able to do. Since a person needs to get over their past before they can move toward their future, cognitive processing focuses on learning about the past and how it shaped that person.

When someone is dealing with their past, it can be quite painful. Therapists who use this method like to take the process slow and find out as much as they can about the past of the person to get the person talking about it and find out what triggers them in the process. This part of learning about the traumatic events or other past issues usually takes around four weeks for a therapist to get through. This is the first stage of the process, and each of the three stages is divided evenly. However long it will take the therapist, and the person who is receiving therapy to get through each of the problems is dependent on this first one and the length of time that it takes.

A therapist will likely ask their patient to come up with ideas about the past. Some people who are going through therapy might find that they actually have repressed memories of the past especially if it was traumatic. This is something that can be detrimental as well as good. While they are trying to get through these repressed memories, they may find something that is the true trigger to their depression and anxiety. It will allow them to see what it is and that they have one which is the first part of getting better and moving forward with their life.

If someone is able to figure out all of their repressed memories and all of the information that they hold, they will be able to learn as much as possible with their emotions and the problems that they have. It will allow them the chance to move on and make their lives better.

Accepting and Processing

Once a person has learned as much as possible about the events in their past and what has created this sort of anxiety or depression state, they will be able to begin the acceptance process. While finding the memories and looking at them clearly was certainly hard during the first step, this can be even harder because they need to "come to terms" with the problems that they had and make sure that they are doing things the right way for their memories.

Once they have taken the time to confront them, they will then need to make sure that they are accepting them. Are they still trying to repress these memories? Or, are they looking them in the face and acknowledging that they are there and they are making problems for the people who need to "get over" the hump of traumatic memories? Once they have learned how to, essentially, look their bad memories in the eye, they will then be able to say that they have officially accepted the memories.

One of the biggest parts of this process is not putting the blame on another person or situation that the person is in while they are repressing memories and trying to recall them. For example, someone may be tempted to think about a traumatic event and blame it on their parents, the person who was with them or even themselves. They need to let go of this blame. They will never have full acceptance of the memory and the trauma that it caused until they are ready to stop blaming someone else, something else or even themselves for the problem. Placing blame with a cognitive processing will not fix the problem or even put a name to the problem, it will just push it further into the context of memories.

As with the first step, it can be expected that this step will take about four weeks. With cognitive processing, therapists do not like to move fast. This is because they need to make sure that each step of the process is being done the correct way and that the patient has moved from one step to the next in the proper way before they can begin it. They will not be able to be successful with any of the steps if they are not able to get through the first or second step.

Getting Through It

Once someone has found the memories and accepted them, they may think that they are out of the woods and that they are healed of their anxiety and depression. This is not the case, though, and it is the point at which many people trip up and lose their own ability to be able to deal with the memories and the things that they have because of them. They need to continue to learn how to *not* repress memories and to keep things light for themselves. It is important to make sure that they know how to get through the situations that they are in and that they are making sure that they will not do it again.

After the cognitive processing is done, the person's brain will be trained to not repress memories and to keep themselves as levelheaded as possible in all situations. The memories that they had, even the ones they did not know about, will no longer be triggers and they will not have to worry about the different problems that come with the triggers. Cognitive processing is effective in that it promotes someone's good memories and allows them to accept the bad while not bringing them up all of the time.

It is important to note that there are many problems that can come with memory repression. This is especially true if someone has anxiety and/or depression due to sexual assault, PTSD or something similar. The memories can be painful and bring them up out of a repressed state can make things even worse for the person. That is why it is important to consult with a mental health professional before trying to do cognitive processing therapy. It can sometimes be detrimental and having the help of a professional will allow the therapy to be more successful.

Chapter 7: Reprocessing and EMDT

Some cognitive behavioral therapy methods work with the mental aspect of the brain while others work with the physical. It can sometimes be hard to cope, especially when anxiety is spiraling out of control. People need to learn how to process that and figure out a coping method that works right for them. The reprocessing therapy works by focusing on the movement of the eyes and how it is able to help a person reprocess all of the information that they have stored in their own brain depending on the different ways that things will be able to go for them and the way that things can be improved when it comes to their abilities.

History

When you are planning on using reprocessing, there are several things that you will first need to take a look at. As with all things that you do in cognitive behavioral therapy, you will need to look into the past to find the memories that can function as triggers for your anxiety and depression. You need to keep track of these memories because this is how you are going to make a change to the triggers that you have the memories that you have made in the past.

Relaxing

You can start to relax the first time that you try to do reprocessing. You will need to take time when you are not stressed about anything and notice the sensations that you feel. Relax your eye muscles, the rest of your head muscles and everything else so that you can make sure that you are getting the most out of the situation. It will allow you the chance to ensure that you are relaxed. Keep track of these feelings. You can then use this when you are having a stressful time.

Cognition Scale

The cognition scale is used to see how well you can relax while you are thinking about memory as a trigger or while there is a trigger that is present and making you tense. It is expected that you would be a 1 or a 2 on the scale when you are first getting started with reprocessing, but by the end of treatment, you should be at the highest point on the scale, a 7. This takes some time and a lot of positive imagery to be able to conquer in the way that you need to start healing.

Retraining

There are several steps to the process, but the retraining part is what you will be able to focus on the most. This is what will make things work the right way for you and will allow you the chance to make sure that you have mastered reprocessing. Once you have learned how to do this, your brain will be trained to immediately start associating the relaxation techniques with the trigger that previously made you feel anxious or upset in any way.

Strengthening

While it may seem that having your brain automatically associate good things with the stimuli you previously experienced in a negative light, this is not always the best way to be able to handle the situation. You will need to learn how to do this in a way that makes more sense and so that you can continue to strengthen the belief that you have that this is, in fact, a positive thing. Doing this will allow you to continue using this technique and will allow you to keep the anxiety at bay for years even after you have finished it.

The easiest way for you to continue strengthening your beliefs is to consistently go back to that place of relaxation. While your brain is still able to do this on its own, you will want to make sure that you do it on a cognitive level as well. You do not need to do this every time that you think that something is going wrong, but when you begin to get stressed or notice stimuli affecting you, you should try to go back to the place of relaxation. There is nothing new to learn when it comes to strengthening, but you will need to remember to practice what you have already learned.

Lingering Sensations

If there are any types of sensations that could cause a person to feel like they are going to become anxious again or that they are going to start to stress, there needs to be a plan in place to be able to handle them. This could be anything from mild stress to tension to need to be surrounded by people or anything else that could signal oncoming anxiety. When a person starts to feel this, they need to take their time and specifically relax for the benefit of themselves. This is the only way that they can get through it.

One thing that many therapists will suggest that their clients do is to go looking for these thoughts and these feelings. When they start to feel a twinge of something bad happening, they need to latch onto that and make sure that they are trying to figure out how to react to it so that they will be able to do more. They can benefit from this because they will be able to learn as much as possible about what makes it happen and what they can do to make it relax. Even years after therapy has been completed, you can benefit from seeking out lingering sensations and quashing them.

Logging It

Throughout all of the different things that go on with reprocessing, you need to log them. You should figure out what you are doing, what you feel and the sensations that you have so that you will be able to learn as much as possible about the different things that are going on. It is important to log it and keep track of it so that you can learn what your triggers are, how to relax through them and how to make sure that you are doing things the right way when you are trying to fix your anxiety and your depression.

Determination

Since you have logged all of the information, it will be easy for both you and your therapist to go back and see what made the determination on whether or not you were going to get anxious over something. You may find that simply logging the information can help with anxiety, but you will need to determine *why* you are anxious, what you have done to fix it and what has worked for you to be able to get through any type of situation or trigger.

The biggest aspect of reprocessing is the physical aspect. Averting your eyes to something else, allowing them to look inward at what you are doing and giving yourself a chance to notice the physical symptoms of what is happening when a trigger is brought to your attention are all ways that you can redirect your own attention away from the different aspects of your life. It is something that you will need to be able to do and use to your advantage when it comes time to continue with the reprocessing and with your own life while trying to overcome the anxiety and depression.

Chapter 8: Rational Therapy Method

The rational look at cognitive behavioral therapy is to make sure that things are being done in a rational way and that the reactions to each of the triggers are handled on a trigger by trigger basis. Rational therapy is a way to make sure that a person reacts in a way that is appropriate instead of an overreaction or a misfire in the reaction to a stimulus that is given.

The Trigger

With rational therapy, the therapist will start by having a subject look at one trigger at a time. Once they are able to overcome one of the triggers, it will then be easier for them to fix the other triggers and they will be able to make sure that they are getting the most out of the situation that they are in without having to worry about the way that the trigger is going to affect them. They will first need to bring up one of their triggers and figure out what happens to them when the trigger is brought about.

Bringing up triggers can be difficult to do when you are not in the situation so if you want to do this, you should be prepared to make a log when you are feeling particularly depressed or anxious. Write down what made you feel that way and what you think did it. If you cannot think of a specific thing on the outside of your head, you can look at the inside of it and see if it was something like an obsessive thought or an intrusive attitude that made you think of the things that you were going to do. It can be anything on the inside *or* the outside of your head that can trigger your feelings.

Stimulating It

Once you have felt that trigger, coax it as much as possible. If you are *trying* to make something trigger you, it can be even harder because the chances of that happening are very slim. The brain will only do it when you are not paying attention and when you are unable to see it coming. Since the triggers can cause organic responses, try to get the triggers to do as much as possible when it comes time to you making sure that things are going the right way and when you are doing different things with your own triggers.

It is a good idea to try to make sure that you can see, physically, what is going on with your response to the trigger. Do you shake? Does your heart rate increase? Do you sweat? Each of these things is responses to triggers and are generally an overreaction of the brain to something that is completely harmless because the brain wants you to think that there is something to be scared of or something that you will not be able to get to when it comes to a certain point. This is known as fight or flight, and it is what you are trying to overcome.

Replacing It

After you have figured out what the trigger is and how it can have a negative effect on you with the different symptoms, try to replace them. Instead of paying attention to your sweaty hands when you see a dog coming toward you on the street, look at a picture of something funny or repeat a mantra to yourself. You can do many different things to replace the negative responses to stimuli but always make sure that they are positive and they are going to be able to help you get the negative response.

It is a good idea to make sure that you are doing the most for yourself by always replacing them with something positive. From the time that you decide that you are going to be rational about your emotions, you can start to replace things that are negative with things that are positive. Instead of telling yourself that you are going to die, tell yourself that you are sitting on a beach and listening to the waves crash. This is the "happy place" technique that many people use when they have to do something uncomfortable, like getting a shot or having to do a scary interview. By figuring out how to get to that "happy place," you will always be able to replace negative emotions.

Perfectionism

Most people who suffer from anxiety and depression do so because they are not able to live up to the standards that they have set for themselves and they do not know how to handle it. They overreact when they are not perfect or when something does not go the exact way that they want it to go. It is something that will not be able to help them and something that will not make a difference in the way that things are done.

When you are able to overcome perfectionism, you will be able to overcome the negative reactive behavior that you have to different stimuli. If you know how to accept things when they are not exactly perfect, you will be able to accept the fact that people do not always do the exact things that they want to be able to do. You may not be able to get the perfect reaction that you want, but you will be able to react in a more rational sense.

Getting rid of perfectionism can be hard especially if that is something that you have always done, but once you conquer this aspect of your life, you will be on your way to getting over the problems that you have with your irrational reactions. It can be difficult to find a balance between not being a perfectionist and being lazy so make sure that you are careful to not go to the other end of the spectrum.

Putting it Into Practice

All of these things will be able to add up and make rational sense to you once you begin to do them. Learn the right way to become more rational before you make the decision to do anything else and that will give you a chance to do better at the way that things are going for your anxiety and depression. It can sometimes be hard to be able to do the same type of things with the way that you are reacting but know that doing that will help you to overcome both anxiety and depression.

Learning how to be more rational and to make emotionally rational decisions will allow you to live a more normal life. Once you take the time to make sure that you are as rational as possible, it will give you a chance to do that when it comes to triggers and other things that are going on in your life. You will find that you will be able to react more normally to triggers than before. You will not need to worry about having to fight or run away from a situation just because that is what your brain is telling you to do. Fixing your brain with anxiety is as easy as learning how to be more rational.

Chapter 9: Dialectical Therapy

As you may have imagined due to the name, dialectical therapy is a type of talk therapy that will allow you the chance to make sure that you are moving forward from the phobias and depressive states that you may get into. This type of therapy is particularly helpful for people who obsess over problems that they may have and for people who want to be able to make sure that they are able to make the right decision. Changing behavior with dialectical therapy is done almost exclusively from within, and it is what some people refer to as mindfulness while using techniques that will teach you more about your inner self.

Looking Around

By taking a minute to look around at your surroundings, you can bring yourself out of your head. While it is important to help yourself with this method inside of your head, you want to be able to do something that will get you out of the behavior that the brain has set up in response to the different stimuli that are all around you. It is important to make sure that the brain is able to do as much as possible with what you are doing and looking at the world around you will give the brain a chance to reset or activate itself to form a normal response.

While you are looking around, you should be talking to yourself (in your head, of course) about what you see.

"I see a steering wheel in front of me."

"There is a dog on a leash."

"My child needs my attention."

Each of these things is looking around you and seeing the way that they are in the world. It will also give you a chance to feel like you are in the world outside of your head.

Reporting

Always report to yourself on what you see. Whether you want to do it all in your head or if you find that keeping a journal is easier when you are first getting started will allow you to remember what you see and what you are going to be able to do in the world around you. It can be difficult to get an idea of what is going on so make sure that you are always working hard to figure that out. The specifics of looking around you can be hard to grasp if you are not making the right type of mental note. Always do your best to figure out what is going on and report it directly to yourself.

Since we are using language and our voice for each of these things, it may be a good idea to consider the voice that you are using. Is it one that is calm and reassured? Or, is it one that is shaky and is making you shaky as well? You can change your voice in your head.

Activating the Response

You can activate the response that you have in your head by taking the time to make sure that you are talking to yourself in the best way possible. Figure out what response you *want* to have to the situation and use that to make yourself get through the situation. It may be hard to do this at the moment so you can always try to replicate the situation in your head. Figure out what you are going to say and what you are going to do if something happens and tell yourself that is what you are going to do.

While the point of any cognitive behavioral therapy is to move on from the past, you may find yourself reverting to the past when you are trying to do this. This can be a problem so make sure that you only use current situations or things that can make it harder for you to think about the past.

Avoiding Binary

As you are looking at the word around you and trying to see different things, it may be easy for you to use judgmental terms about the things that you are seeing. You may look at a child who dropped their ice cream cone and say to yourself that is unfair. You should try to avoid this, though.

Make sure that you are looking at all of it subjectively. Instead of thinking that it is unfair, think that the child dropped their ice cream cone and that is it.

It can be hard to do this and do not get discouraged if you cannot do it at first but looking at everything subjectively will give your brain a chance to reset and look at everything for what it truly is instead of for the unfairness of it all. Doing this can allow you the chance to make sure that your brain looks at stimuli in a subjective manner.

Focusing on One

If you happen to notice that you cannot stop the inner dialog from moving to something negative, try your hardest to focus on one thing that is positive. This will be the best way for you to be able to get things done and will allow you the chance to make sure that you are getting the best response possible.

When you think about it, this is what your brain does anyway. If you see a dog coming toward you, the only thing that you can think about is a dog attack and what you will look like after it or how bad it will hurt. Instead of doing this, when you look at a dog, think about something positive. Think about how much the owners probably love the dog and continue focusing on that *one* thing. Doing this will allow your brain to switch off the fight or flight response and will slow it down to think more rationally.

Radical Acceptance

When you find that you have a bad response to stimuli or you are being triggered, you should be able to handle the problem by using different techniques. If you are unable to do this, radical acceptance can help. For example, if you are driving and think that you are going to have a heart attack, give into it. Convince yourself that you have one and that you are going to die and then accept it. This is radical, but it is something that will nearly always work. If you take the fear away from something, it takes power away from it too.

Self-Soothing

When you are unable to calm yourself using *any* of the other techniques, you can try some type of self-soothing. This is a skill that is established when people are babies and when they are left to cry for a certain amount of time. They learn to calm themselves through different things, and it allows their thought process to work out the solution to the problem. Whether your self-soothing technique is rubbing a certain spot on your wrist or tapping your feet or even doing something somewhat unhealthy like licking your lips, you can try different things that allow you to soothe yourself when you are scared or worried about something.

Conclusion

Thank for making it through to the end of this book, I hope it was informative and was able to provide you with all of the tools you need to achieve your goals whatever they may be.

The next step is to figure out which cognitive behavioral therapy technique is going to work the best for you and your mental health and start implementing the strategies and take action.

Here's to your success!

Thank you!

Before you go, I just wanted to say thank you for purchasing my book.

You could have picked from dozens of other books on the same topic but you took a chance and chose this one.

So, a HUGE thanks to you for getting this book and for reading all the way to the end.

Now I wanted to ask you for a small favor. **Could you please take just a few minutes to leave a review for this book on Amazon?**

This feedback will help me continue to write the type of books that will help you get the results you want. So if you enjoyed it, please let me know! (-:

www.ingramcontent.com/pod-product-compliance
Lightning Source LLC
Chambersburg PA
CBHW081145020426
42333CB00021B/2673